KING GUEZO OF DAHOMEY

uncovered editions

Series editor: Tim Coates

Other titles in the series

uncovered editions

KING GUEZO OF DAHOMEY, 1850–52

THE ABOLITION OF THE SLAVE TRADE ON THE WEST COAST OF AFRICA

∞≈⟐≈∞

London: The Stationery Office

© The Stationery Office 2001

All rights reserved. No part of this publication may be
reproduced, stored in a retrieval system, or transmitted in any
form or by any means, electronic, mechanical, photocopying,
recording or otherwise, without the prior permission of the
publisher.

Applications for reproduction should be made in writing to
The Stationery Office Limited, St Crispins, Duke Street,
Norwich NR3 1PD.

ISBN 0 11 702460 0

Abridged. The full-length edition was first presented to
Parliament in 1852 as *Papers Relative to the Reduction of Lagos by
Her Majesty's Forces on the West Coast of Africa*.
© Crown copyright

A CIP catalogue record for this book is available from the
British Library.

Cover photograph © Hulton Getty: Dahomey, 19th century
(14327568)

Typeset by J&L Composition Ltd, Filey, North Yorkshire.
Printed in the United Kingdom for The Stationery Office by
Biddles Ltd, Guildford, Surrey.
TJ3345 C30 2/01

About the series

Uncovered Editions are historic official papers which have not previously been available in a popular form. The series has been created directly from the archive of The Stationery Office in London, and the books have been chosen for the quality of their story-telling. Some subjects are familiar, but others are less well known. Each is a moment in history.

About the series editor, Tim Coates

Tim Coates studied at University College, Oxford and at the University of Stirling. After working in the theatre for a number of years, he took up bookselling and became managing director, firstly of Sherratt and Hughes bookshops, and then of Waterstone's. He is known for his support for foreign literature, particularly from the Czech Republic. The idea for *Uncovered Editions* came while searching through the bookshelves of his late father-in-law, Air Commodore Patrick Cave OBE. He is married to Bridget Cave, has two sons, and lives in London.

Tim Coates welcomes views and ideas on the *Uncovered Editions* series. He can be e-mailed at timcoatesbooks@yahoo.com

SELECTED GLOSSARY

barracoon	a slave warehouse, or an enclosure where slaves are held temporarily
bight	bend in the coast forming an open bay
cabooceer	superintendent of trade
charchar	agent
cowries	brightly coloured shells, used as currency in Dahomey
cruizers	battleships
emoluments	profits
felucca	small boat
immolations	sacrificial killings
krooman	African employed on board ships
levee	assembly, reception
palaver	long parley or discussion
plenipotentiaries	envoys entrusted with special negotiating powers
prolix	lengthy
specie	coined money

Although the British abolished the slave trade in 1807, and the actual institution of slavery in 1833, the slave trade continued to flourish along the west coast of Africa (popularly known as the Slave Coast) until the the mid-19th century. Part of the problem lay with the African chiefs who continued to sell their own people into slavery, obtaining European merchandise in exchange for captives taken during tribal wars.

King Guezo of Dahomey was one of these African chiefs who, while being very friendly towards the British, had no intention of giving up his war-like habits. With 18,000 royal wives, 3,000 Amazon women in his army, and a warrior-like reputation to maintain, he could see little attraction in farming as an alternative lifestyle. For entertainment, he would regularly indulge in human sacrifice.

Lord Palmerston was Foreign Secretary conducting affairs from Britain at the time of these delicate negotiations between the British Consul and the African chiefs. Just how the British managed to coerce them into abandoning their lucrative trade is revealed in fresh and fascinating detail by these contemporary despatches.

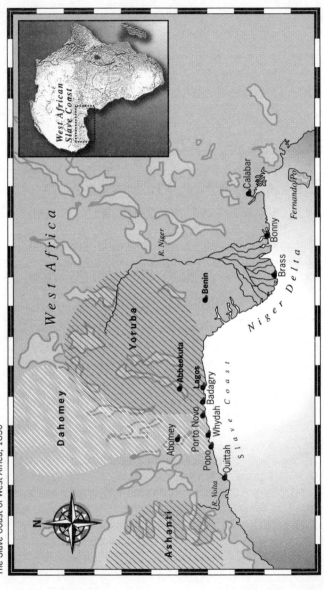

The Slave Coast of West Africa, 1850

JUNE 1849

Viscount Palmerston to Consul Beecroft

(Extract)   *Foreign Office, June* 30, 1849

Representations having been made to Her Majesty's Government from time to time by persons engaged in legal trade in the Bights of Benin and Biafra, stating that it would be desirable that a person should be appointed to reside in that part of Africa as agent on the part of Her Majesty's Government, for the purpose of regulating the legal trade between British merchants and the ports of Benin, Brass, New and Old Calabar, Bonny, Bimbia, the Cameroons, and the ports in the territories of the King of Dahomey, Her Majesty's Government have determined to make such an appointment; and being informed by the Commodore commanding on the west coast of Africa, that it will be agreeable to you to hold it, I have to inform you that the Queen has been graciously pleased to confer that appointment upon you, and that a commission under the sign manual will be prepared accordingly, and will be transmitted to you at the same time with this despatch.

You have been selected for this appointment in consideration of your general knowledge of African affairs and of the habits of the Blacks, and because of the influence which you appear to have acquired over the native chiefs of the places to which your Consular jurisdiction will extend. That influence, it is hoped, may enable you to prevent quarrels and misunderstandings between those chiefs and the crews of British ships resorting to those parts for the purposes of trade; and thereby, on the one hand, legal commerce will be promoted, while, on the other hand, the Slave Trade, which can scarcely co-exist with legal commerce, will be much discouraged.

With a view to these results, you will endeavour to encourage the chiefs and people to till the soil and to produce available exports, so that they may obtain by barter the European commodities of which they may stand in need.

You will take every possible opportunity to impress upon the minds of the chiefs and their principal councillors, the great advantages which they will derive from the extension of legal commerce with the nations of Europe and America; and you will assure them that Her Majesty's Government earnestly desire to contribute to their welfare and improvement.

You will transmit to me, from time to time, the best information which you can procure as to the means by which commercial intercourse with the chiefs on the coast and in the interior can be extended, and as to the points of the coast which may appear to afford the greatest facilities for commerce; and you will also state what kinds of European commodities are most sought after by the natives.

It will be your duty at all times to keep up a cordial intercourse and good understanding with Her Majesty's naval officers on the West African station, and to communicate to them any information which may come to your knowledge from time to time respecting the Slave Trade; and Her Majesty's naval commanders will be instructed to afford you every facility and assistance in their power to aid you in the performance of your duties.

You will receive in other despatches general instructions for your guidance in your Consular functions, and also in matters relating to the Slave Trade.

Viscount Palmerston to Consul Beecroft
Foreign Office, June 30, 1849

Sir,

I transmit to you letters which I have addressed to the several chiefs on the western coast of Africa, within the district of your Consulship.

You will take a convenient opportunity to present these letters to the chiefs on the coast, when you will explain to them the nature and object of your appointment. I enclose a copy of the said letter.

PALMERSTON

Enclosure
Letter to be delivered to African chiefs

The Queen of Great Britain and Ireland, my Sovereign, has commanded me to acquaint you that Her Majesty has been graciously pleased to grant a commission appointing Mr John Beecroft, the Governor of the Island of Fernando Po, to be Her Majesty's Consul to the several chiefs on the western coast of Africa.

It will be a principal duty of Mr Beecroft to endeavour to prevent the frequent misunderstandings which have arisen between the chiefs on that coast and the British merchants, and the crews of British vessels resorting to those parts for the purposes of trade; and he will also be instructed to encourage and promote legitimate and peaceful commerce, whereby the chiefs and people may obtain in exchange for the products of their own country, those European commodities which they may want for their use and enjoyment.

In this manner the great natural resources of your country will be developed; your wealth and your comforts will be increased; and the detestable practice of stealing, buying, and selling men, women, and children, which is now the bane and disgrace of Africa, will be put an end to.

The Queen's Consul is instructed to take every suitable opportunity to explain to you the great advantages which you will derive from the increase of a legitimate commerce; and he is instructed to assure you of the earnest desire of the Queen's Government to contribute in every way to your welfare and prosperity.

The Queen trusts you will receive Her Majesty's Consul with the respect due to his character and rank, and that you will put entire faith in what he shall state to you in Her Majesty's name.

PALMERSTON

JANUARY 1850

Viscount Palmerston to Consul Beecroft
(Extract)   *Foreign Office, January* 23, 1850
Lieutenant Forbes, of Her Majesty's Navy, and the late Mr
Duncan, who had been appointedVice-Consul in Dahomey,
went up in October last from Whydah upon a mission from
Her Majesty's Government to the King of Dahomey. The
object of their mission was to induce that African chief to put
an end to the Slave Trade in and through his dominions, and
Mr Duncan delivered to him two letters, of which the
enclosed are copies, urging him to do so, and setting forth
arguments to show that by so doing he would promote,
instead of injuring, his own interests and those of his subjects.

You will be furnished with copies of the despatches
from Lieutenant Forbes and from Mr Duncan, giving an

account of their proceedings while employed on this service, and of what passed between them and the King of Dahomey; and I have to request that you will make yourself acquainted with their contents.

You will see by those despatches that Lieutenant Forbes and Mr Duncan were most kindly and hospitably received by the Dahomey Chief, and that they were assured by him of his sincere and anxious desire to secure for himself the friendship and good-will of the Queen of England, by following, as far as it is possible for him to do so, any advice which Her Majesty's Government might give him; but he said that the profits which he derived from the Slave Trade constituted a considerable part of his revenue, and to put an end to that Traffic would be to sacrifice a material portion of his income. He said that, therefore, he must have time for full consideration and mature deliberation before he could answer the letter which Mr Duncan had delivered to him; but that if Lieutenant Forbes and Mr Duncan would come back to him, as he requested they would, at his next annual Custom in March of this year, he would then be prepared to give his answer to Her Majesty's Government.

As Mr Duncan has been unfortunately lost to Her Majesty's service, I have to instruct you to accompany Lieutenant Forbes on his return to Dahomey, being satisfied that your judgment and discretion, together with your practical knowledge of the character and habits of the African races, peculiarly fit you for the performance of this duty. You will therefore proceed in Her Majesty's ship "Sphinx", which will convey you direct to Whydah, where it is probable that you will find Lieutenant Forbes; but if he should not be there he will be sent for, and you will await his arrival, which will not be long delayed, and you will in any case, immediately on your landing at Whydah, send up to the King of Dahomey to inform him of your arrival on the coast and of your intended visit to Dahomey.

You will proceed to Dahomey as soon as Lieutenant Forbes and yourself can set out for that place together.

If on your arrival at Dahomey, the King should declare himself ready to enter into the engagement which was proposed to him for the abolition of the Slave Trade in and through his dominions, you will, of course, at once proceed to conclude with him a treaty to that effect. But the likelihood is that he will hold to you about the Slave Trade the same sort of language which he held on that subject last October to Lieutenant Forbes and Mr Duncan; that he will profess his anxious desire to comply with the wishes of Her Majesty's Government, but will plead financial considerations as reasons why it is impossible for him to do so.

In that case you will endeavour to explain to the Chief that the profits which he derives from the Slave Trade are precarious in their nature and limited in their extent. That they mainly depend upon the presents which the slave-dealers on the coast may be able to make to him, or upon duties paid to him on the passage of slaves through his territory, or on the price which he may obtain for captives taken in those warlike expeditions, the cost of which must in some measure absorb the profit which he may make by selling his prisoners. That the continued measures of various kinds which the British Government are taking with a view to suppress the Slave Trade tend every year more and more to hamper the transactions of the slave-traders established on the coasts of his territory, and thus to diminish progressively the means of those slave-traders to make him presents or to pay duty on the passage of slaves through his dominions, or even to purchase the prisoners of war whom he may wish to sell. That, on the other hand, his territories abound with resources for legitimate trade, and that if he was to employ his great power and authority for the encouragement of legitimate commerce, as a substitute for the Slave Trade, he would very soon find that he would derive from moderate and reasonable customs duties a much greater and far more certain revenue than he at present receives from the Traffic in Slaves. Such legitimate commerce the British Government would use every proper endeavour to encourage and protect, and the interest of the King of Dahomey in regard to such trade would be identical with that of the British Government; and the States of Dahomey and Great Britain, instead of being, as now, kept in some degree on different courses, in regard to their supposed interests, in consequence of their different views and opinions with respect to the Slave Trade, would be drawn together in close bonds of union by their common feelings and mutual interests in regard to the protection, encouragement, and extension of legitimate commerce.

The foreign merchants established at Whydah are already beginning to see the great advantages which are to be derived from legitimate commerce; and whereas some years ago they were almost all of them engaged, chiefly if not entirely, in the Slave Trade, it appears that now they almost all of them have dealings in the palm-oil trade nearly as extensive as the dealings which they have in the Slave Trade.

But palm-oil, though a commodity much valued and wanted in Europe, and the exportation of which from Africa to Europe has been yearly increasing, is not the only produce of that part of Africa which could be the subject matter of extensive and profitable commerce between Dahomey and Great Britain. Cotton of excellent quality might be produced in almost any quantity within the territories of Dahomey, and any quantity of cotton there produced would find a ready and profitable market in the manufacturing districts of the United Kingdom. The cotton so sent to Europe would of course be paid for by such European commodities as might suit the wants and tastes of the people of Dahomey, and moderate customs duties levied upon the importation of such commodities would soon afford a considerable and an increasing revenue to the King.

But the King of Dahomey might probably object that the loss which he would sustain by the suppression of the Slave Trade would be certain and immediate, while the profit which might accrue to him from import duties on legitimate trade would be uncertain, and at all events not arising until after some lapse of time.

To obviate this objection, if made, you are authorized to say that if the King of Dahomey would immediately and entirely put an end to Slave Trade in and through his dominions, the British Government would engage to make him for a limited time, say three years, an annual present as a compensation for the loss which he would during that period sustain, it being reasonably to be expected that by the end of such a time legitimate commerce would have afforded him an income which would fully make up to him for the loss incurred by the cessation of Slave Trade. Her Majesty's Government must leave it to your discretion to make with the Chief the best arrangement which you can on this head, and you are authorized, in case of necessity, to promise an annual present, either in money or goods, at the option of the King, to be continued for three years.

If you can conclude a satisfactory arrangement, on this principle, you will draw up and sign with the King a treaty to that effect.

You will express to the King of Dahomey the deep concern felt by Her Majesty's Government at the death of the late Mr Duncan, a concern which they are convinced is fully shared by the King, whose kind and friendly conduct towards Mr Duncan afforded Her Majesty's Government the highest gratification; and you will say that Her Majesty's Government hope to be able to appoint some fit and proper person to be Vice-Consul in Dahomey in the place of Mr Duncan.

You will of course transmit to me a full report of all your proceedings in the execution of these instructions, and when this service has been completed, and when proper opportunities offer, you will visit the different chiefs in the neighbouring country to whom you are accredited as Her Majesty's Consul, and you will present to them respectively the letters which I have addressed to them by the Queen's commands, and which are enclosed in my despatch of the 30th of June, 1849, explaining to them at length the nature and object of your appointment, as described in your general instructions.

After these services shall have been performed, and when other and more immediate duties will permit, you will at a suitable season proceed on a mission to Abbeokuta, for which I will furnish you with instructions in another despatch.

Enclosure 1
Viscount Palmerston to the King of Dahomey
Foreign Office, May 29, 1849

The Queen of Great Britain and Ireland, my Sovereign, has commanded me to acquaint you that Her Majesty has been graciously pleased to direct Mr John Duncan, the bearer of this letter, to reside for the present in the territories of Dahomey as the British Vice-Consul.

It will be a principal duty of Mr Duncan to endeavour to prevent the misunderstandings which may have arisen between the chiefs on the coast of Dahomey and the British merchants and the crews of British vessels resorting thither for the purpose of trade; and he is also instructed to encourage and promote legitimate and peaceful commerce, whereby the chiefs and people may obtain in exchange for the products of their own country, the European commodities which they may want for their use and enjoyment.

In this manner the great natural resources of your country will be developed; your wealth and your comforts will be increased, and the detestable practice of stealing, buying, and selling men, women, and children, which is now the bane and disgrace of Africa, will be put an end to.

The British Vice-Consul is instructed to take every suitable opportunity to explain to you the great advantages which you will derive from the increase of a legitimate commerce; and he is also to assure you of the earnest desire of the Queen's Government to contribute in every way for your welfare and prosperity.

Her Majesty's Government trust you will receive the British Vice-Consul with the respect due to his character and rank, and that you will put entire faith in what he shall state to you in the name of Her Majesty's Government.

PALMERSTON

Enclosure 2

Viscount Palmerston to the King of Dahomey
Foreign Office, May 29, 1849

The Queen of Great Britain and Ireland, my Sovereign, commands me to acknowledge the receipt of your letter dated the 3rd of November [see next paper], which I have laid before Her Majesty, and to thank you for your friendly assurances. The British Government is glad to find that you wish the Slave Trade to be put an end to in all places beyond the limits of your territories, because that wish on your part shows that you are sensible of the bad nature of that Trade.

With regard to your own dominions, you may be quite certain that if you would stop the Slave Trade, and if you were to encourage legal commerce instead of Slave Trade, your revenue and the profits of your people would not be diminished, but would very shortly be much increased; for it is well known that agriculture and commerce are more useful and advantageous than the stealing and selling of men, women, and children.

With respect to the other matters touched upon in your letter, I will write to you on another occasion.

I avail myself of the return of Mr Duncan, whose appointment as Vice-Consul in your dominions I have notified to you in another letter of this day's date, to send to you a few articles of British manufacture, which Mr Duncan informed me you had expressed a desire to have, and which Mr Duncan will deliver to you as a present from Her Majesty's Government.

PALMERSTON

Letter from the King of Dahomey to Her Majesty Queen Victoria, alluded to in the preceding.

Abomey, November 3, 1848

The King of Dahomey presents his best compliments to the Queen of England. The presents which she has sent him are very acceptable, and are good for his face.

When Governor Winniett visited the King, the King told him that he must consult his people before he could give a final answer about the Slave Trade. He cannot see that he and his people can do without it. It is from the Slave Trade that he derives his principal revenue. This he has explained in a long palaver to Mr Cruickshank. He begs the Queen of England to put a stop to the Slave Trade everywhere else, and allow him to continue it.

The King is anxious that the Queen of England should send a Governor to Whydah Fort, in order that he may have an opportunity of seeing the manner in which the King governs his people.

The King also begs the Queen to make a law that no ships be allowed to trade at any place near his dominions lower down the coast than Whydah, as by means of trading-vessels the people are getting rich, and withstanding his authority. He wishes all factories for palm-oil removed from Badagry, Porto Novo, Agado, and Lagos, as the trade that is now done at these places can be done at Whydah, and the King would then receive his duties, and be able to keep these people in subjection; and also in the event of his attacking these places he would not run the risk of injuring Englishmen or their property.

He hopes the Queen will send him some good Tower guns and blunderbusses, and plenty of them, to enable him to make war. He also uses much cowries, and wishes the Queen's subjects to bring plenty of them to Whydah to make trade. He wishes to see plenty of Englishmen making trade at Whydah.

The King has spoken all his mind to Mr Cruickshank, who can explain what is fit for the King and his country. He begs the Queen of England to continue his good friend, as he likes Englishmen more than any other people.

Enclosure 3
The King of Dahomey to Viscount Palmerston

Abomey, September 7, 1849

I, Guezo, King of Dahomey, beg to return my sincere thanks to the Queen of England and Lord Palmerston, for presents sent to me by them, through Mr Duncan. I beg also to thank Lord Palmerston for his good advice respecting the trade of this country, and I do assure Lord Palmerston that the earliest opportunity will be taken of consulting my Cabooceers on the subject, and at the next annual Custom held here, Mr Duncan shall be made acquainted with our decision. I have always a strong desire to cultivate a friendship with the people of England, and to establish and increase a trade with that country. Englishmen were my father's best friends, and he always told me to respect Englishmen, and look upon them in my heart as sincere in their promises and friendship. An Englishman's heart is big, like a large calabash (gourd) that overflows with palm-wine for those who are thirsty. I know that the Portuguese and Spaniards care nothing for me, their friendship and presents are all to serve their own purpose of obtaining slaves, upon which they themselves derive the principal profit.

I beg to thank Lord Palmerston for appointing my friend, Mr Duncan, Vice-Consul for my country, and I promise to protect and assist him in performing the duties for which you have placed him here, and shall afford him the same protection when passing through my country, as I did on his last journey in my dominions. I have broken the Dassa Country, whose people went to war against Mr Duncan when passing their country. I hold their chief a captive ever since ten moons after Mr Duncan's visit to their country, and have kept him in my house, that Mr Duncan might see his enemies in captivity before he die; he has now seen him, and my heart rejoiceth. And so shall fall every one who shall molest an Englishman while under my protection.

I am much pleased with the proposal of cultivating cotton in my country, and have already planted the seeds given to me by Mr Duncan. Mayo has also planted some. I beg to assure the Queen of England and also Lord Palmerston, of my sincere friendship and gratitude.

Signed (Mayo holding the top of the pen) on behalf of Guezo, King of Dahomey,

MAYO LADYETTO, *Prime Minister*

[Read over three times, at the request of the King.]

Enclosure 4

Commodore Fanshawe to Lieutenant Forbes

(Memorandum)   *"Centaur", Loanda, September* 9, 1849

Mr Duncan, recently appointed by Her Majesty's Government to be Her Majesty's Vice-Consul within the dominions of the King of Dahomey, being about to proceed on a special mission from Whydah to the King's capital, has represented to me that His Majesty has sent three times to him, expressing to him a wish that he might be accompanied by a naval officer; and considering that a compliance with the King's wish may give additional importance to Mr Duncan's mission, and further the views of Her Majesty's Government with reference to the suppression of the Slave Trade, I have decided to permit a naval officer to accompany him, and I have selected you for the purpose, provided you feel equal to undertaking the journey, as an officer who has had now considerable experience on the African station, and acquired some knowledge of the native languages and habits. You will therefore put yourself forthwith in communication with that gentleman at Whydah, and in case of your accompanying him, you will be guided in your conduct and interview with the King of Dahomey, by the following instructions, in as far as, on conference with the Vice-Consul, you find they are in no respect at variance with those he may have received from Her Majesty's Government.

You will be prepared to appear at his Court in the full-dress uniform of your rank, and in every respect to maintain the character of a British officer.

You will be strictly guarded in all your intercourse with the native chiefs and others, to give no cause of offence, bearing in mind their superstitious character and habits.

You will make it your first object to support the position of Mr Duncan as the Diplomatic Agent of Her Majesty the Queen.

The Slave Trade without doubt has been long and actively pursued within the Kingdom of Dahomey, and the power and wealth of the King, and the extent of his dominions, has enabled him to supply the dealers on the coast to any amount. Your next great object will be to obtain the most accurate information in everything connected with that question.

The recent death of the wealthy Brazilian slave-dealer, Da Souza, at Whydah, who has been supposed to be an agent of the King of Dahomey, and to have had some influence with him, appears to afford a favourable opportunity of approaching the King again on the subject of the abolition of the Slave Trade within his dominions. You will therefore avail yourself of any opportunity in conference with him or his chief people, to impress them with the greater benefit they must derive from retaining their people in their own country for the cultivation of the soil, and the extension of commerce by the exchange of its products for articles of European manufacture and general legal trade, than by the cruelty of selling them to a slave-merchant, to be carried away to enrich another country; and you will endeavour to explain to the King and chief people, that the great desire of your Sovereign and her people is to see Christianity introduced into every part of Africa, and thereby to increase the civilization, welfare, and happiness of her people; and that knowing that the great benefits of peace and commerce have been the happy results in all those parts where the Slave Trade has been abolished, and general trade for the produce of the country introduced, Her Majesty would receive with much pleasure any intimation from the King of Dahomey, of his desire to do the same, and make a treaty with her for the purpose.

You will also assure the King and his chiefs, that it would be a great satisfaction to me if I could be the instrument of promoting the wishes of my Sovereign, and of effecting such a treaty on the part of Her Majesty with them, and thereby establish a cordial and lasting good understanding between the Sovereigns and people of both countries; and if you succeed in attracting attention to the subject, you will endeavour to ascertain the King's view, and on what terms he would be disposed to execute any such treaty. I hardly expect he is so prepared at present; but I furnish you with blank Forms of treaties such as have been concluded with the African chiefs, for your guidance, and authorize you to act, in case any opening is afforded you, to their extent.

You will thank His Majesty for the countenance and support already afforded to the English and American missionaries who have come to reside within his country, for the sole object of promoting the happiness of his people, by the introduction of the Christian religion, and beg his continued protection of them; and, if opportunity is afforded, you will express to the King how contrary the practice of human sacrifice is to the principle of that religion, and how gratifying it would be to your Sovereign the Queen to know that the King had ordered it to be discontinued within his dominions.

I hope Mr Duncan may be able to accomplish the object of his mission quickly, and that you may be able to return in three weeks to Whydah; at any rate you must not let your absence be prolonged unnecessarily beyond that time. You will prepare and forward to me a full and detailed report of all your proceedings, and of any expenses incurred; and, on your return to Whydah, you will receive orders from the senior officer of your division for your further guidance.

Before leaving Abomey you will inquire for any reply from the King to my letter.

ARTHUR FANSHAWE

Enclosure 5

Vice-Consul Duncan to Viscount Palmerston

(Extract)   *Whydah, September* 22, 1849

I have the honour to acquaint you of my safe arrival at
Abomey, the capital of the Kingdom of Dahomey. I started
from Whydah on the evening of the 24th of August, and
arrived in Abomey on the 30th; we rested one day at
Canamina to prepare for our entry and reception in the
capital. We were very tired from excessive fatigue in passing
through the swamp between Ahguay and Ahgrimmy. It is
nine miles across, and during this season of the year it is
almost impassable

At the entrance to the capital we were met by all the
principal Cabooceers and officers of the household; after
the usual ceremony of drinking healths with all of them,
accompanied by a continual fire of musketry, we were conducted to the Palace; and after passing by three times in
parade-order, the King requested me to dismount and
come to him. I found him the same frank, unassuming, but
intelligent man I had found him in 1845. He expressed his
great satisfaction at seeing me once more, according to my
promise, and said he hoped that the Queen of England had
sent me to live at his hand for a long time, and to teach his
people some of the arts of civilized life. He next inquired
of the Queen's health, and the whole of the Royal Family
of England; next the Queen's Cabooceers, and then drank
the Queen's health, and afterwards her Ministers', accompanied by roars of musketry.

The King was dressed in a plain cotton robe, without
any ornament. He was surrounded by his female soldiers,
some of them very good-looking; and some of the younger
ones nearest his person were very richly dressed and
ornamented.

Nearly all of the female commanders recognized me;
they stood up alternately, making each a long speech

complimentary of my return, expressing their readiness to sacrifice their lives to serve me, as the friend of their King. At this moment the old Chief of Dassa was brought before me a prisoner; the fine, venerable old man appeared so terror-striken as to be almost unconscious of what was passing. The King told him his prophecy had now been fulfilled. He, the chief, had with his people turned out to attack one solitary white man, in a country where he had no father, no mother, except the King of Dahomey, who would always be a father to Englishmen; and also endeavoured to force a guard which accompanied him, although capable of annihilating the whole of the Dassa people. The King told him to look around him, and see the female soldiers who so easily conquered his country; he also told him he was now at my discretionary disposal. I dared not ask for his liberty, but was promised he should only be detained as a State prisoner. He was very clean, and seemed to want for nothing. It was now getting late in the afternoon, and the King gave us leave to depart.

Two days after, the Queen's presents were got ready, and sent to him through Mayo. The King was much pleased with the presents, especially with the scarlet uniforms and scarlet cloth. He was also much pleased with a spinning-wheel sent by my mother from Scotland, and also with a small model weaving-loom I had made for him. He requested me to show him how to spin, which placed me in rather an awkward position, especially as it was cotton instead of flax. However, I acquitted myself to his satisfaction. After overhauling the edge-tools, and inquiring their particular uses, he requested that I should take some of them back to Whydah, for the purpose of instructing two young men whom he promised to send down here under my charge.

On the day previous to my departure from the coast for Abomey, the King sent a messenger to acquaint me that it will be necessary, holding office in his dominions, that I shall attend his annual Custom; in consequence of which I kept some few of the presents for that occasion, having plenty of other articles of hardware, which I added and presented in the name of Her Majesty. This will enable me to go full-handed on my next visit, when he promises to give me full answers to your Lordship's letter respecting the Slave Trade. He listened very attentively to the letter, and said that when I attend his Custom, and see the quantity of money he pays to his people annually, I shall be better able to give an opinion whether legitimate trade can be extended to afford a revenue equivalent. I told him it was probable some years must elapse ere that could be done. He must himself call forth the resources of the soil of his country; and told him, that as cotton was the spontaneous production of the soil, it could easily be increased to any extent, and we would purchase as much as he chose to raise. This proposal seemed to please him very much. He admits there is no market for slaves now, which makes him very poor indeed. He promised to do all in his power to extend the cultivation of cotton, provided I remain in his country and secure a market for it. The King admits the injustice of slave-trading, but remarked that we were a long time finding it out to be wrong; and as soon as he finds that by any other means he can raise sufficient revenue, he will readily abandon it; but again remarked he would answer all at the next Custom.

On the 6th of September the King sends Mayo with a variety of presents for myself and companions—1 fine young cow, 3 goats, 6 fowls, 3 bags of native flour, 3 kegs of fine palm-oil for cooking, 3 measures of pepper, and 3 kegs of rum, besides 3 fine native cloths.

During our sojourn in the capital, we were entertained at the King's expense. After sunset Mayo came to acquaint us that it was the King's desire that we should drink, before we leave the capital, the Queen of England's health. This, of course, was readily agreed to; and accordingly we followed Mayo to an open space in front of English House, where we found a table already laid out in real English style, and covered with a cloth I had presented a day or two before. Mayo filled the glasses with water, first, which is customary, being considered a sincere mark or pledge of friendship, being pure and unadulterated. They were next filled with wine; and Mayo proposed the health of Queen Victoria of England, which was followed by a "hip-hip-hurrah!" which passed along a line of half a mile of men stationed for that purpose. Immediately the hurrah ceased, a salute of twenty-one guns was fired in honour of Her Britannic Majesty, with a degree of regularity that would do credit to more civilized nations. This was followed by nine guns in honour of myself as British Vice-Consul.

The kind reception of the King of Dahomey has excited a great degree of jealousy on the part of the Spanish and Portuguese slave-dealers, consequently they look upon me with great suspicion since my return from the capital.

On Saturday last the Custom commenced, according to the country usage, for the late Don Francisco da Souza, who died on the 8th of May last; he was the Charchar, or Mayor of the Spaniards and Portuguese in Whydah. Great anxiety prevails at this moment amongst his sons as to the decision of the King in appointing a successor. It is expected the second son will have it; he is considered the best man as far as regards disposition and qualification; but it is expected that the Government of Whydah will not be carried on with the same energy as before.

The Custom is likely to last a month; a great nuisance in the town, as continual firing of ordnance and small arms is irregularly kept up, with drums of the most barbarous kind, day and night, Sunday not excepted, I forgot to mention.

It is with much satisfaction I am enabled to inform your Lordship that all the gibbets exhibited in the market-places in Abomey on my former visit are now done away with, and the skulls placed on the walls by the former King are suffered to decay without being replaced. This is one step towards civilization.

I have this day been visited by some respectable people from Ahguay, who some years ago emigrated from Sierra Leone; they appointed their headman to come here to present a petition, which I have enclosed to your Lordship. Cole, the bearer to me, is a very respectable man, and expresses his own and the whole of the Sierra Leone people's readiness to assist me in carrying out any agricultural experiment, and in collecting and planting cotton: this would assist these people themselves, as well as employing them profitably to those requiring their services. They are despised by the slave-dealers, as their presence and their education tends to expose the slave-dealing system. Nothing will afford me more gratification than to be the means of doing good for my country, and entirely abolishing Slavery on this part of the coast, and establishing a system of remunerative industry and an extension of legitimate commerce.

Enclosure 6
Lieutenant Forbes to Commander Harvey
(Extract)   *Whydah, October 6, 1849*
I have the honour to state that yesterday Mr Duncan and myself had an interview with the Cabooceer (Governor), the French merchant (M. Blancheley) attending, and at the request of the Cabooceer, Mr Hastie also.

The Cabooceer sent for Mr Duncan and myself this morning and we were received most politely.

A messenger was instantly sent to the King to acquaint him of my arrival, and it appears to be necessary that we should wait until his return, before leaving this, that being the custom of the country, and any attempt to oppose such custom would at least give great offence.

It would appear that the Customs to the memory of Da Souza are drawing to a close, and that the King has sent to inform the Portuguese merchant Domingo Martinez, now living at Porto Novo, that if he will come to Abomey he shall be received as Charchar, but he is only to come on condition that he settles at Whydah, which it is not expected he will do, as he is carrying on a lucrative trade there.

We cannot now start before Wednesday or Thursday, but as everything will be ready by the return of the messenger, no delay will take place after his arrival. I do not apprehend a lengthened delay at Abomey in consequence of the absence of the Cabooceers, but Mr Duncan is of opinion that the King will be much pleased with his wishes being so minutely attended to, and be better prepared to conform with the wishes of the Government at the Customs.

Enclosure 7
Lieutenant Forbes to Commander Harvey
Whydah, October 11, 1849

Sir,

I have the honour to state that last evening at 7 o'clock the King's messenger returned, bearing His Majesty's stick, and a request that Mr Duncan and myself would immediately proceed to Abomey. It was delivered by the Cabooceer's headman, on his knees, and face on the dust.

Every opposition that can be has been made by the Portuguese merchants, luckily without any serious consequence; but the difference of reception to what ought to have been offered to me on landing was yesterday illustrated on the arrival of a Portuguese supercargo (I believe of a slave-vessel), who landed a few days back at Popo, and reaching the King's custom-house at Whydah by a lagoon, was met by all the Cabooceers and some 500 soldiers, who saluted him.

Great excitement prevails among the Portuguese merchants as to the cause of my mission, and several expedients have been tried, without effect, to discover its purport.

The greater part of our goods go to-day, and we proceed to-morrow; when we return is of course uncertain, but I do not expect to be more than twenty days from this date.

F. E. FORBES

Enclosure 8

Lieutenant Forbes to Commodore Fanshawe

(Extract)   *"Bonetta", at sea, November* 1, 1849

Pursuant to your orders dated September 9, 1849, I have the honour to lay before you a full and detailed report of my proceedings on a journey to Abomey, the capital of the Kingdom of Dahomey, on such matters as are of interest to Her Majesty's Government, written in the form of a journal.

October 3, 1849. Arrived at Whydah; found at anchor Her Majesty's ship "Kingfisher".

Commander Harvey having explained to me the difficulties (reported to the Commander-in-chief) he had encountered in communicating with Her Majesty's Vice-Consul, I proceeded to the back of the surf, and sent a Kroo canoe with three Kroomen, to ascertain its extent and exact state. The Kroomen effected a landing; but in attempting to return, the canoe was broken in pieces.

October 4. Having borrowed the Kroo canoe belonging to Commander Harvey, I entered her at the back of the surf, still very high, but had no sooner attempted to land, than the canoe was capsized and broken; after much danger, assisted by the three Kroomen who landed yesterday, I swam on shore.

October 5. Visited the Viceroy. Having been introduced by Mr Duncan, and having explained my views, the Vice-Consul took advantage of the opportunity to explain to the Viceroy that the French house of Blancheley had offered him the keys of the French Fort for transmission to the King (they intending to return to France), unless their trade, which had been stopped, was reopened. Mr Hastie, agent for Hutton and Co., who was present at the Viceroy's request, in a most unwarrantable manner, stated that unless the French trade was reopened, the men-of-war would enforce it. I instantly desired Mr Hastie to be silent; yet the threat was no sooner made, than the Viceroy rose in a furious passion, saying, "If you wish to break this country, you can do so: go! go!" He then retired; but entering a few minutes after, pointing to me, he asked why I remained. I told him I was waiting until his passion was over, to shake hands with him, and to explain to him that he must be labouring under a false impression, if he imagined either Mr Duncan or myself had hinted any threat. This cooled him, and shaking hands, I left the house.

October 6. The Viceroy sent at an early hour to desire an interview with the Vice-Consul and myself. On arriving at his house, we were ushered into a private apartment, and soon explained how much he had been mistaken in Mr Duncan's intentions. I am of opinion that yesterday the Viceroy was inebriated, and possessed with a false impression of our intentions. I am fully aware that Mr Hastie had told him that Mr Duncan was a private individual, formerly a soldier, and now passing himself off as a Consul, without authority. I gleaned from Mr Hastie's own words that he had hinted to the Viceroy that I had no further claim to a visit to Abomey than that of an officer on leave; and to prove it, he, the Viceroy, should demand to see my papers before he allowed me to proceed. In consequence of the above, I had provided myself with my instructions, which I produced unasked. Mr Hastie had to pay a fine for his interference; such fines, in the idiom of the Dahomian language, are termed "wiping the mouth".

After much conversation, the Viceroy assuring me that he now understood the Vice-Consular position, begged, in the idiom of the language, that "the palaver might be set", to which I consented, or, in other words, not to mention again the insult of yesterday. He now received my seal to send to the King to ask permission for me to proceed to Abomey.

October 7. I inspected the British Fort, which is in a most disgraceful state of want of repair, and unworthy the name it bears; the guns all dismounted, and the walls in a dilapidated state. By a letter shown me to-day by Mr Hastie, the firm of Hutton and Company, London, claims the property of the Fort, and in consequence their agent has placed Mr Duncan and his two countrymen in two apartments totally inadequate to their wants. Their agent retains the key of the Fort, and shows no respect to the Vice-Consular authority; on the contrary, strives in every way in his power to draw down the ridicule, not only of the native authorities, but also of the Portuguese and other merchants, and, as far as he is able, to render Mr Duncan's residence as uncomfortable as he can to himself, and his official position nugatory [worthless]. The British Fort has, I am informed, never been repaired at the expense of Messrs Hutton, but by the King obliging the English town people to work at a nominal subsistence, paid by Messrs Hutton as a moderate tax.

In Dahomey all preliminaries are settled by presents, and I witnessed a disbursement on the part of Don

Domingo Jozé Martins, of goods to the amount of 5,000 dollars, most of them given, I understood, to counteract any injury my visit might have caused to the interests of the slave-merchants.

The public square (Whydah) ran with rum from three pipes started for the mob to wallow in. Thirty-five pipes of rum besides silk and cowries (the currency of Dahomey) were sent to the King. The Viceroy and all the Cabooceers were large receivers. These presents are common to all slave-merchants, and the late Senhor da Souza is said to have paid 1000*l.* annually (in goods) besides presents. At this moment, except Domingo Martins, there are none who can afford large gifts.

In Whydah there are a great number of returned slaves (liberated Africans) from Sierra Leone and Bahia. This day (Sunday) all were gaily dressed, the Bahians walking to and from church; but the Sierra Leone people told me with regret that they had no church.

In the whole Kingdom of Dahomey there is but one Christian place of worship, the Catholic chapel of the Portuguese Fort. The religion of the Dahomian is of the worst order of paganism, worshipping a snake of the boa constrictor species.

The French Fort is in a most respectable state of repair. The Portuguese one moderately so.

October 8. The Viceroy visited me officially, attended by a company of soldiers, who kept up a constant independent fire during the interview, as a salute to me. During the conference he begged I would report to the British Government the dilapidated condition of the Fort, and the imperfect state of its batteries. He was very condescending, and particularly civil.

October 9. Mr Hastie has raised a report that the Portuguese merchants charged him with having given information to

Commander Harvey, whereby Her Majesty's ship "Kingfisher" captured a slave-brig. He having reported the same to Commander Harvey, that officer empowered me to contradict it; but on inquiry all the respectable merchants declared they never hinted such a charge. It was most probably invented to lead me to suppose he (Mr Hastie) was entirely independent of the slave-merchants.

October 10.This day, the supercargo of a slaver having landed at Popo, arrived, and was received by the Viceroy in state, under the fire of some hundreds of musketry. After meeting him at the end of the town, the Viceroy paraded the whole of Whydah, attended by the Cabooceers under huge painted umbrellas, and accompanied by band of music and standards.

In the evening the messenger returned from the King, commanding that I should immediately proceed to Abomey, attended by Mr Duncan. As protection he sent his stick, a gold-headed Malacca cane, which was presented to me by the Viceroy's headman, with his head on the ground, and throwing dirt on his head.

October 11. Hired bearers, sixteen for hammocks, and twenty men and women to carry cowries, rum, and baggage, and sent the latter on the road.

October 12. Visited the Viceroy on leaving, who received the King's stick, and having prostrated himself, and placed dirt on his head, returned it to me, adding that with that I wanted no protection, but to supply my wants and assist me as a linguist, he gave me his hand and foot, his headman, Narwhey.

October 13. Arrived at the royal city of Allahdah, having passed through a fine park country, intersected by corn and ground-bean farms; not a pebble or stone of any kind is to be seen between this and Whydah, twenty-eight miles. At

Allahdah one human skull is exposed, that of a man found in the royal harem.

On the fifth day of our journey we arrived at the royal city of Canamina, or Camioh, and thence sent a messenger to inform the King of our arrival. The country passed has been very regular and level, except in the neighbourhood of an extensive swamp, about fifty miles from Whydah, where there is a slight irregularity. In the vicinity of this swamp there is much ironstone, sandstone, and conglomerate. It is surrounded, and has been the bed of a lagoon or river, and bears every appearance of a coal deposit. In the afternoon the messenger returned.

October 17. Started in full uniform for the capital, distant ten miles. Having entered the gate of the city, which is ornamented with human skulls, and in the vicinity of the principal Fetish-house, we halted, and taking position in chairs across the road, waited for the ceremony of being met by the Cabooceers. In a short time an immense crowd advanced towards us, with banners flying among them.

At some distance they halted, and the Governor of the city, at the head of a few soldiers, advanced. When arrived in front of our position, he countermarched, and made a circle from left to right three times round our seats, bowing each time he came in front. On the last time he fired off a musket, and danced before us; then having shaken hands, took a seat.

One of the King's brothers next performed the above ceremony; then a band of the royal household, chanting a welcome, followed by other Cabooceers; lastly two regiments of musketeers and one of blunderbussmen; these last having passed, commenced an independent fire, while we were regaled with spirits and water sent by His Majesty. The whole then re-formed in procession, and entering our hammocks, they preceded us to the Palace-yard.

The square in front of the Palace, though extremely large, was densely crowded with armed men and women squatted on their hams, their long Danish muskets standing up like a miniature forest. Scores of banners of all colours and devices added to the scene, those of the King surmounted by a skull.

The Palace wall, of red clay, standing about twenty-five feet high, extending over more than a square mile, was one continued line of human skulls, yet it might be remarked that where decay had destroyed, these ghastly ornaments were not replaced; on the thresholds and sides of the portals of the Palace were also human skulls; but the practice of human sacrifice is fast vanishing from the Kingdom of Dahomey.

The palaces of Dahomey are extensive harems, entered only by the King and eunuchs, except at the Customs, when they are thrown open to the inspection of all visitors.

In the centre of the wall open upon the square is a huge gateway over which a roof is built, under this, on a mat, lay the King. The gates thrown open discovered at least 3,000 of the royal wives richly dressed, while immediately around the Monarch stood his Ministers, Cabooceers, and favourite wives, magnificently attired.

Notwithstanding the vast concourse in the square, the ground was well kept, marked out by bamboos; a road was formed round the square through which we were carried three times, still preceded by the Cabooceers, who each time they passed the King prostrated and threw dirt on their heads; etiquette simply required us to bow. After the third round we left our hammocks, and, still preceded by the chiefs, slowly approached the King, who now rose to receive us. When within a few paces the Cabooceers made a lane and again prostrated and kissed the dust; through this lane we advanced and shook hands with the King.

King Guezo is about forty-eight years of age, good-looking, with nothing of the negro cast of countenance, his complexion wanting several shades of being black; his appearance is commanding, his countenance intellectual, though stern. That he is extremely proud there can be no doubt, for he treads the earth as if it were honoured by its burden. Contrasted with the gaudy attire of his Ministers, wives, and Cabooceers (of every hue), laden with ornaments of coral, gold, silver, and brass, the King was plainly dressed in a loose robe of yellow silk slashed with satin stars and half-moons; he wore Mandingo sandals, Spanish hat trimmed with gold lace; the only ornament being a small gold chain of European manufacture.

Having taken seats round the Royal mat we soon entered into a complimentary conversation, the Prime Minister whispering into the Royal ear, the interpreter not being allowed to address the King directly in matters of compliment.

The King now introduced me to his Ministers: Mayo, Prime Minister; Meigau, of Police; Cambodee, Treasurer; Maehaepah, Justice; Toonoonoo, Eunuch-in-chief; then to an elderly lady called the English Mother, named "Yawae", one of the matrons of the harem who provides food for English visitors. Next all the Cabooceers were introduced.

The King then expressed a wish I should witness a review of female troops, and two regiments were at once paraded, but not before the ground was shifted and marked out for the manœuvring. The officers (female) distinguished by armlets of silver reaching from the wrist to the elbow, and carrying each a small whip. The whole were uniformly dressed in tunics of blue and white, armed with a musket, club, and short sword, carried cartouch-boxes, and went through several evolutions, skirmishing, firing volleys, etc. with much precision. After the review the officers were introduced and complimented.

The King next proposed Her Majesty the Queen of England's health, which he said he knew we preferred to drink in champagne, which we did accordingly; but as the King drank it several screens were held before him, as mortal may not gaze on His Majesty either in the act of eating or drinking.

After drinking His Majesty's health also in champagne, we were permitted to take leave. The King accompanying us across the square, where all now was animation: the thousands of armed men and women rushing round their Monarch, brandishing aloft their clubs and muskets, and yelling and shouting in a most fearful manner.

Our quarters were in the Prime Minister's enclosure, a recently built house for English visitors.

October 18. At an early hour we were commanded to appear before the King, and I was directed to bring my despatches.

After much delay and ceremony, we were ushered into a small apartment, immediately within the Palace gate; on a bed covered with a mat and satin pillows, reclined the King, who rose to receive us; there were present the Prime Minister, a few of the ladies of the harem, and some five attendants, besides Mr Duncan and the two interpreters. I immediately proceeded to business.

Having presented the Commander-in-chief's letter [of introduction], the King desired me to read it to him, which I did in short sentences, explaining their meaning; and causing them to be translated by both interpreters at the same moment, who often appeared to be correcting each other, and thus probably giving the King a true version.

Having finished the letter, I read those portions of my instructions which referred to the Slave Trade, Mr Duncan's position, human sacrifices, and the introduction of missionaries. Concerning the Slave Trade the King intends answering at the Customs; Mr Duncan's position the King understands; human sacrifices I felt I could thank him for having so far reduced in numbers; the introduction of missionaries he courts.

Having gone into much detail on the advantage of legal trade, of the probability, in consequence of increased coercion on the part of the Brazilian Government, of his not deriving high profits in future from the sale of slaves, when I had written the King's letter to the Commander-in-chief, the public business was closed.

We conversed for some time on various topics, and among others, the King's wish that the Slave Trade should be stopped in the neighbouring States.

After drinking a great deal of champagne, we took leave, accompanied to the end of the square by the King. At the moment he had stepped out of the Palace, not a soul was to be seen, but before we parted, thousands had surrounded, armed as yesterday, and thousands more were rushing from all sides, shouting, and brandishing aloft their weapons.

The markets are very extensive, in which foreign as well as native goods of all kinds are exposed for sale; there being no shops, these markets, or fairs, are the only places where articles are bought and sold; they take place once in five days, and in the neighbourhood of Abomey there are several, so that each day there is a market.

October 19. At an early hour assembled outside the Prime Minister's house, to hear a salute of twenty-one guns fired in honour of Her Majesty the Queen of England, nine as a salute to myself, and nine in honour of Mr Duncan. After drinking Her Majesty's health, the troops hurrahed, and the salute commenced; but before it was half-over, we were all obliged to scamper after the Prime Minister, and hide our faces against the wall, as a portion of the 18,000 royal wives were passing, ringing a small bell, as these sable ladies are all over the town at all times, and no male may gaze on them unpunished.

The salute over, the King's permission was given us to depart when convenient, and as a return for my present, the Prime Minister presented in the King's name a large country cloth for the hammock (so expressed), 20,000 cowries for the road, some flour, palm-oil, peppers and a bullock, which had not arrived when Her Majesty's ship sailed.

The King was at an expense of no less than 200 dollars in consequence of our visit; food in enormous quantities was sent daily for our consumption.

October 20. Quitted the capital; the Vice-Consul unwell with dysentery.

October 25. Arrived at Whydah. Mr Duncan much worse. Took lodgings in the town.

October 26. Senhor Domingo Jozé Martins sent to offer his boats for my embarkation. This offer saved me much inconvenience, as Senhor Martins, although a slave-merchant, is in part a legal merchant also. It is absolutely necessary that the Vice-Consul should have the means of communicating with Her Majesty's ships; he should be provided with at least two large canoes and a set of canoe-men (twenty).

October 29. Her Majesty's ship "Kingfisher" arrived.

October 30. The surgeon of Her Majesty's ship "Kingfisher" having decided it necessary, embarked the Vice-Consul, Mr Duncan, very ill with dysentery.

Her Majesty's ship "Kingfisher", at noon, fired a royal salute in honour of the King of Dahomey, and in answer to the salute to Her Majesty the Queen of England, fired at Abomey.

Arrived Her Majesty's ship "Bonetta". Rejoined, and sailed for Liberia.

Enclosure 9

Lieutenant Forbes to Commodore Fanshawe
"Bonetta", at sea, November 5, 1849.

Sir,

I have the honour to lay before you the following report on the existing state of the Slave and other trades in the Kingdom of Dahomey.

Guezo, the present King, some years ago, at the wish of his subjects, deposed his brother Adonooza, the latter having fallen into the degrading habit of inebriation.

Guezo no sooner became King than he made it his chief policy either to employ his people in war or amuse them with festivals. In order to ensure success in the former (and as it will be seen in both) he established large armies of male and female soldiers, and in the course of time conquered the Kingdoms of Anagoo, Mahee, Bassa, and Kangaroo, thus rendering Dahomey a large monarchy. Instead of being tributary (as formerly) to the Kingdom of Ashantee, he has placed that country nominally at his feet, sent his defiance, and built a palace under the name of Coomassee (that of the capital of Ashantee) to commemorate the declaration.

Besides minor there is one annual festival known as the Customs, which takes place on the appearance of the third moon, March 13, 1850, and lasts six weeks. To this festival the whole of his subjects are invited, also all foreigners, traders, and others, sojourners in his kingdom, and all are assembled at the expense of the King. In order to defray this enormous expense, the King makes war on one or the other neighbouring countries, and performs what is termed a "slave-hunt". These hunts the King always superintends, and in order to excite emulation, gives the female soldiers a different portion to overrun from the male; in the performance of which duty the females almost always excel.

The King having acquired a taste for European articles of merchandise, has a great desire to strengthen his alliance with foreigners. Having no doubt of their national protection, he holds the British and French people in great respect, while, on the contrary, although he admits that the Portuguese, *i.e.* slave-merchants, readily purchase all his slaves, he treats them with much contempt, forcing them to pay many additional duties, etc.

The Kingdom of Dahomey, although of such vast inland extent, has but one seaport, Whydah, or more properly *Greogwei*, the Dahomian name, while the slave-merchants term it *Ajuda*. From the number of slave-merchants residing at Whydah, that port is strictly watched by the cruizers. Of these merchants the late Da Souza, a Brazilian, was the chief, or Charchar, friend and agent to the King. Although Da Souza was at one time said to possess 120,000,000 dollars, at his death he was almost a pauper, the consequence of having been over liberal in his presents, and having met with some severe losses at sea. Besides the enormous expenses of his household, his wives alone amounting to 300, he lived in great magnificence, every article of table or domestic use was of solid silver.

Of the sons of Da Souza there are three wealthy slave-merchants; the eldest, Isidore, is a resident of Popo, and will become Charchar magistrate of slave-merchants, if Domingo Martins declines that office. The other two are Antonio Cockoo and Ignacio.

Domingo Jozé Martins, the richest merchant in the Bights (Brazilian), is a resident at Porto Novo, where he commands a monopoly of both slave and palm-oil trades, each of which he works to an enormous amount, and he is the only merchant in the Bights that ships a whole slave cargo; the others club their slaves, and ship in proportion to their means all in one or more vessels. Martins has a large consignment of British cotton on palm-oil account at Porto Novo. He has an establishment also at Whydah.

Joaquim Almeida, the richest resident in Whydah, was originally from the Mahee country; sold into slavery, he has returned from Bahia, and is now a slave-merchant on an extensive scale.

Jacinta, a native of Madeira, and Jozé Joaquim, fill up the number of Brazilian and Portuguese merchants; the latter was formerly a private soldier of the Brazils. There are also many petty dealers. The house of Joaquim Antonio is the only Spanish firm.

By means of lagoon the slaves can be shipped at either Porto Novo, etc., to the eastward, or Popo, etc. to the westward, with much greater safety; but as these ports are the property each of a neighbouring chief, the King of Dahomey is jealous of his slaves being shipped without his kingdom, as thereby he loses the head-tax of 20 dollars, a heavy sum; and hence his repeated desire the Slave Trade might be put a stop to in the neighbouring States, and shipments allowed in Whydah.

The price of a slave, from the trade being almost a royal monopoly (or at least a Martins one), is very high, being (in goods) from 80 to 100 dollars. Hence with many captures there is great loss; the consequence is, that each slave-merchant counteracts the chances of the losses in some degree, by embarking also in the palm-oil trade, and at this moment not one slave-merchant in Whydah but works both trades.

The French house of Blancheley is working a large palm-oil trade. There are a few supercargoes of Hamburgh vessels generally residing, who invariably purchase through Portuguese or Brazilian agency.

The Americans have no trade at Whydah.

Hutton and Co., the only British firm, as far as I can judge, are not purchasing.

The resources of the country might be much extended, the soil is capable of producing all tropical plants, sugar corn, fruits, etc., though the curse of the locusts is felt at times. The timber is magnificent at a little distance from Whydah. The animal kingdom is well furnished. The geologist and the botanist would find ample employment and be well repaid for developing the hidden treasures of the Kingdom of Dahomey. The exports at once might be palmoil, cocoa, and ground-nut oil, timber, Indian and Guinea corn, cotton and yams (to the rivers). The jealousy of the present trade removed, there is no part of Africa where stock and even luxuries can be produced so abundantly and cheap. The manufactures are cloths of various kinds and pottery.

At this moment the King is prepared for a slave-hunt, but *ad interim* he is performing the festival in memory of his mother, at which large numbers of his subjects and all his soldiers are assembled.

The seat of war will be in the country of Anagoo, situated to the westward of Abomey; this country has already been subjugated by the Dahomians.

The King thus states his reasons. That in the reign of his grandfather, the Anagoos invested [besieged] Abomey, and so closely that the women could not leave the city for water (which is procured from a distance of six miles), without fear of being kidnapped. The consequence was, great suffering on the part of the Dahomians; neither his grandfather nor his father were fighting men, but quietly submitted to the ravages of the inroad. He had, however, conquered the Anagoos, but did not consider them as yet sufficiently punished; that he must have money (slaves for the ensuing Customs), and he thought of all his hereditary enemies, the Anagoos most deserved the chastisement.

The fact is, he has conquered almost all his neighbours, and is at a loss for some new field in which to perform his slave-hunt. Malefactors are mostly punished with death, but may be reprieved and sold into slavery. Domestic slaves are on no account allowed to be sold into foreign slavery. Should a merchant allow a slave to become a parent in Dahomey, he cannot sell either parent or child into foreign slavery. Slaves are never exposed in the market, but all sales are arranged privately in the houses of the dealers.

The shipments of the last six months, independent of those captured, are as follows: from Porto Novo, 3 with 570 slaves; 1 with 200 slaves; 1 with 300; 1 with 70: all schooners, the two former built for the Trade, the latter a French vessel, purchased. Report speaks of two other schooners, but I failed in getting particulars. From Whydah 1 with 200 slaves (a schooner fore and aft), built for the Trade. From Popo 1 with less than 100 slaves, a French schooner purchased. Report states that three others have lately shipped, but again no particulars. From River Volta, 1 with 200 slaves, a schooner built for the Trade. From Lagos and Jaboo I have no information, but in Her Majesty's ship under my command, chased unsuccessfully one schooner laden (reported).

The slaves in hand at this moment are as follows: at Abomey the King has two cargoes, but I have failed in discovering of what amount; at Whydah 50 slaves; Popo, 800; Porto Novo, none; Lagos, unknown.

At Whydah the jealousy of the trade revealed that the Spaniards have established themselves at Formosa, working the Nun and Brass Rivers, and that a felucca [small boat] had escaped full. Such is the case, and the felucca escaped the "Waterwitch" and "Phœnix" about six weeks since.

The merchants in the Volta and to the westward of Cape St Paul's are Spaniards.

F. E. FORBES

FEBRUARY 1850

Viscount Palmerston to Consul Beecroft
Foreign Office, February 25, 1850

Sir,

I now proceed to give you instructions for your mission to Abbeokuta, to which I alluded in the concluding part of my preceding despatch.

A short time since a deputation from the Church Missionary Society waited upon me, and represented among other things that the establishment of commercial relations with the interior of Africa through the Yoruba tribe, would materially contribute to the suppression of the Slave Trade, and that if free and secure navigation on the Ogu could be obtained, most of the advantages which were proposed by the expedition of the Niger in 1842 would be attained; that traders from the banks of the Niger visit the principal markets of Abbeokuta; and that there is little doubt that the road to Egba and Rabbah, the former of which was the highest point reached by the Niger expedition, might be opened for trade through the Ogu River.

Abbeokuta, as I am informed, is the chief town of the Egba province of the Yoruba Kingdom, and contains above 50,000 inhabitants. It is situated upon the east bank of the Ogu, and that river is navigable for canoes to within a mile of Abbeokuta, and discharges itself into the sea at the Island of Lagos. Lagos is therefore said to be the natural port of Abbeokuta; but the Slave Trade being carried on at Lagos with great activity, the Yoruba people have been obliged to use the port of Badagry, between which and Abbeokuta communications are carried on by a difficult road by land.

But besides the impediments which the slave-dealers at Lagos throw in the way of legitimate commerce, the Yoruba people experience another hindrance to their prosperity, and a constant cause of alarm from the hostility of the King of Dahomey, who harasses them by an annual slave-hunt, and who is said to have threatened the destruction of the town of Abbeokuta. His enmity is said to be especially excited by the fact that the Yorubas are becoming prosperous and are gaining wealth by their commerce with the English, and by refraining from Slave Trade.

The Yorubas are represented to be a commercial people in their habits, and much trade has been carried on between Abbeokuta and Sierra Leone, by way of Badagry. It is also believed that many of the liberated Africans have emigrated from Sierra Leone to Abbeokuta, and many vessels owned entirely by liberated Africans are said to be employed in the Trade between Sierra Leone and Badagry. There is also a regular trade carried on between London and Badagry. English missionaries have been received both at Badagry and Abbeokuta with great kindness, and their valuable services in imparting religious instruction and in promoting social improvements appear to be duly appreciated by the natives. The people of Abbeokuta are said to feel a strong desire that the Slave Trade should be wholly abolished, and that legitimate traffic should be substituted for it; and the Egba chiefs manifest a favourable disposition towards the English nation.

Under these circumstances, Her Majesty's Government have deemed it advisable that you should at a suitable season visit Abbeokuta, in order to ascertain by inquiry on the spot, the actual wants, and wishes, and disposition of the Yoruba people.

I have accordingly to instruct you to proceed on this mission as soon as you conveniently can. Before you proceed, however, to Abbeokuta, it will be advisable that you should first visit the chiefs on the coast within your Consular jurisdiction, and that you should endeavour to ascertain the sentiments and intentions of such of them as have not already entered into amicable relations with Great Britain.

You will explain to those chiefs what is stated in my letters addressed to the chiefs themselves, that the principal object of your appointment is to encourage and promote legitimate and peaceful commerce, whereby those chiefs and their people may obtain in exchange for the products of their own country, those European commodities which they may want for their own use and enjoyment; so that the great natural resources of their country may be developed, their wealth and their comforts increased, and the practice of stealing, buying, and selling men, women, and children, may be put an end to; and you will impress upon their minds that it is the earnest desire of the Queen's Government to contribute in every possible way to their welfare and prosperity, if they will but listen favourably to your overtures, and will honestly follow the friendly counsel which is offered to them by the British Government.

When by personal communication with these chiefs, you shall have made yourself acquainted with their disposition, and shall have ascertained how far they may be inclined to break off their connection with slave-dealers, and to apply themselves to legitimate trade, you will be the better prepared to undertake with advantage your mission to Abbeokuta.

With respect to any aggressive intentions of the King of Dahomey towards the Yoruba people, you will have an opportunity, during your visit to Abomey, to bring that subject under the notice of the King; you will represent to him that the people who dwell in the Yoruba and Popo Countries are the friends of England, and that the British Government takes a great interest in their welfare, and would see with much concern and displeasure any acts of violence or oppression committed against them; that, moreover, there are dwelling among those tribes many liberated Africans and British-born subjects whom Her Majesty's Government are bound to protect from injury.

It is to be hoped that such representations as these, enforced by whatever influence you and Lieutenant Forbes may have acquired over the King in the course of your negotiations upon other matters, may induce the King to make a formal promise to abstain from future aggressions against the people of Yoruba and Popo, and from molesting in any way the liberated Africans or Europeans who reside in Abbeokuta and Badagry, or who frequent the countries adjoining the territories of Dahomey.

PALMERSTON

Enclosure

*The President of the Church Missionary Society to Sagbua and
other Chiefs of Abbeokuta*

I have had the honour of presenting to the Queen the letter of Sagbua and other chiefs of Abbeokuta, and also their
present of a piece of cloth.

The Queen has commanded me to convey her thanks
to Sagbua and the chiefs, and her best wishes for their true
and lasting happiness, and for the peace and prosperity of
the Yoruba nation.

The Queen hopes that arrangements may be made for
affording to the Yoruba nation the free use of the River
Ogu, so as to give them opportunities for commerce with
this and other countries.

The commerce between nations in exchanging the
fruits of the earth and of each other's industry is blessed by
God.

Not so the commerce in Slaves, which makes poor and
miserable the nation which sells them, and brings neither
wealth nor the blessing of God to the nation who buys
them, but the contrary.

The Queen and people of England are very glad to
know that Sagbua and the chiefs thinks as they do upon this
subject of commerce. But commerce alone will not make a
nation great and happy like England—England has become
great and happy by the knowledge of the true God and
Jesus Christ.

The Queen is therefore very glad to hear that Sagbua
and the chiefs have so kindly received the missionaries, who
carry with them the Word of God, and that so many of the
people are willing to hear it.

In order to show how much the Queen values God's
word, she sends with this, as a present to Sagbua, a copy of
this word in two languages, one the Arabic, the other the
English.

The Church Missionary Society wish all the happiness and the blessing of eternal life to Sagbua and all the people of Abbeokuta.

They are very thankful to the chiefs for the kindness and protection afforded to their missionaries, and they will not cease to pray for the spread of God's truth, and of all other blessings in Abbeokuta and throughout Africa, in the name and for the sake of our only Lord and Saviour Jesus Christ.

CHICHESTER

Viscount Palmerston to Consul Beecroft
Foreign Office, February 25, 1850

Sir,

I herewith transmit to you a letter which I have addressed to the King of Dahomey, explaining generally the nature of your appointment as Her Majesty's Consul in the Bights, and the objects of your journey to his capital; and I have to instruct you to deliver it to the King.

I enclose a copy of the letter in question for your information.

PALMERSTON

Enclosure

Viscount Palmerston to the King of Dahomey
Foreign Office, February 25, 1850

The Queen of Great Britain and Ireland, my Sovereign, has commanded me to inform you that she has been graciously pleased to grant a commission appointing John Beecroft, Esq., to be Her Majesty's Consul to the several chiefs of Africa whose territories lie between Cape St Paul, at the western extremity of the Bight of Benin, and Cape St John, at the southern extremity of the Bight of Biafra.

It will be an important part of Mr Beecroft's duties to endeavour to prevent misunderstandings from arising between the chiefs of that part of Africa, or their dependents, and Her Majesty's subjects, either residing in or resorting to those parts for the purpose of lawful commerce.

Mr Beecroft will be accompanied in his visit to you by Lieutenant Forbes, with whom you are already acquainted, and they are instructed to propose to you a formal Treaty for the abolition of Slave Trade within your dominions; and to explain to you the advantages which you and your territories would derive from the increase of lawful trade, and further to assure you of the earnest desire of the Queen and her Government to contribute in every way to your welfare and prosperity.

Mr Beecroft will reside at the Island of Fernando Po; and he will make periodical visits, as occasion may require, to the territories of the several chiefs to whom he is accredited. He is further instructed to take charge of and to forward to Her Majesty, or to Her Majesty's Government, any communications which you may have to make to them. He will confer with you as to the best means of developing the resources of your country and of increasing the lawful commerce of your dominions, and of thus adding to the wealth and comforts of yourself and your people.

The Queen trusts that you will receive Mr Beecroft with the respect due to his character and rank, that you will put entire faith in what he shall state to you in her name, and that you will extend to him your protection, while within the limits of your dominions.

PALMERSTON

APRIL 1850

Consul Beecroft to Viscount Palmerston (received June 15)
"Kingfisher", off Porto Novo, April 8, 1850
My Lord,
I have the honour to communicate my safe arrival off
Whydah yesterday at noon, and communicated with
Captain Harvey, in command of the Bights Division. I was
extremely sorry to learn that Commander Forbes had
sailed in Her Majesty's brigantine "Bonetta" for Ascension,
four days before our arrival.

In consequence of a communication from the King of
Dahomey to Commander Forbes, that his yearly Customs
intended to be kept in March, were postponed until the
middle of May, that he had not any desire to receive visitors
before that period; I was transferred with the presents for

the King of Dahomey on board of Her Majesty's brig "Kingfisher". Her Majesty's steamer "Sphinx" left under steam for Ascension at 3 o'clock.

Under the present circumstance of the case, I deemed it prudent to proceed as soon as possible to my head-quarters, Fernando Po, taking with me the presents to be delivered by me to the King of Dahomey, according to your Lordship's instructions, on my visit at his annual Customs.

Captain Harvey has been very kind, and will order Her Majesty's steamer "Phœnix", Captain Wodehouse, to take me to head-quarters, and to return to Whydah by the 15th of May, by one of Her Majesty's vessels; it will enable me to arrange affairs at Fernando Po, and to visit some of the chiefs of the rivers in the Bight of Biafra, before I depart for Abomey, for I expect to be absent two or three months.

It is reported on shore at Whydah, that the King has been unsuccessful in his last marauding expedition; that three or four of his principal chiefs have been captured by the enemy, which misfortune has no doubt perplexed a man of such an unconquerable spirit. I imagine it is the main cause of the postponement of his Customs until the 15th of May. I understand he is very anxious to ransom them before he commences his parade and feast. I think my proceedings will meet with your Lordship's gracious approbation.

JOHN BEECROFT

Lord Eddisbury to the Secretary of the Admiralty
Foreign Office, April 22, 1850

Sir,
I have laid before Viscount Palmerston your letter of the 8th instant, enclosing a copy of a letter from Commodore Fanshawe [not included here], transmitting the Treaty concluded on the 2nd February last with the Chiefs of Gallinas

and Solyman, for the abolition of the Slave Trade; and I am in reply to request that you will state to the Lords Commissioners of the Admiralty, that Lord Palmerston is of opinion that the next step which it seems desirable to take with a view to clear the African coast north of the Equator from Slave Trade would be to induce the Chief of Lagos to conclude a similar Treaty, and a rigid watch upon his port might probably bring him to agree to do so.

EDDISBURY

JULY 1850

Commodore Fanshawe to the Secretary of the Admiralty
"Centaur", West Bay, Prince's Island, July 19, 1850
Sir,

I have to request you will do me the honour to lay before the Lords Commissioners of the Admiralty, the accompanying copies of a letter and journal which I have received from Lieutenant Forbes, of Her Majesty's brigantine "Bonetta", detailing the particulars of his late mission with Mr Beecroft to the King of Dahomey, with a statement of the expenses incurred by him.

Although the mission has not had an immediate satisfactory result, I still entertain a hope that it may lead to measures which will cause the abolition of the Slave Trade in the King's dominions.

The decision and intelligence manifested by Lieutenant Forbes on this occasion, quite confirm the opinion which caused me to select him for the service, first to accompany the late Mr Duncan, and I beg therefore to recommend him as an officer deserving their Lordship's approbation.

Lieutenant Forbes is the bearer of Mr Beecroft's despatches to the Foreign Office, and also of a letter from the King of Dahomey and a present from him of two country cloths to Her Majesty the Queen.

ARTHUR FANSHAWE

Enclosure 1
Lieutenant Forbes to Commodore Fanshawe
"Bonetta", West Bay, Prince's Island, July 8, 1850

Sir,

In enclosing my journal reporting my proceedings on my late mission to Dahomey, I have the honour to state that, May 14, I landed at Whydah with Mr Consul Beecroft, and arrived at Abomey, May 26, where I remained six weeks. Returned to Whydah and re-embarked, July 12, on board the "Bonetta", and resumed the command of her.

Having had several interviews and conversations with His Majesty the King of Dahomey and his Ministers, I have formed the following conclusions:

1st. That the King of Dahomey will not give up the Slave Trade without some show of coercion.

2nd. That His Majesty's Ministers are one and all slave-dealers; and if the King was willing, he has not the power to treat.

3rd. That His Majesty's wealth has been much exaggerated.

4th. That there is no Dahomey nation, but a few chiefs holding feudal rights under a high chief,

Guezo. The case of John McCarthy, mentioned in my journal of proceedings, will point out the fear entertained of the stoppage of all trade.

His Majesty's recommendations to the Queen to stop the trade in the ports from Quittah to Lagos, illustrates the efficiency of such a demonstration on Whydah.

The King is about to make war on Abbeokuta. Mr Beecroft and myself have explained to him that in Abbeokuta dwell many British subjects; and that Sagbua, the Chief, has sought British protection.

If it were represented to King Guezo, that if he makes war on Abbeokuta he declares war upon England, it would perhaps save Abbeokuta, or enable you to stop the trade at Whydah, which, if the King does not open by relinquishing the Slave Trade, will in a very short time ruin the country.

A present of powder and musket-balls would raise the confidence of the Abbeokutians.

F. E. FORBES

Enclosure 2

Journal of Lieutenant Forbes, on his mission to Dahomey (Extract)

May 13. Arrived off Whydah, and embarked on board Her Majesty's ship "Phœnix", where I had the honour of being introduced to Mr Beecroft.

May 14. Landed, surf rather high, one chest of muskets: twenty lost. Her Majesty's ship "Kingfisher" saluted, twenty guns. British Fort saluted as we entered the town of Whydah.

May 15. 6 AM, visited Viceroy, and introduced Mr Beecroft as Her Majesty's Consul, and explained to him our position as Her Majesty's Plenipotentiaries. Took private apartments in the British Fort.

May 17. Viceroy called. He starts on 20th; we are to start 21st. Isidore da Souza is Charchar; Ignacio da Souza, Cabooceer; Antonio da Souza, Amigo del Rey; three appointments out of one that their father enjoyed—the reason obvious: His Majesty receives three presents.

May 21. Sent on baggage. At 5 started, and at 9 arrived at Torree.

May 22. Arrived at Allahdah. In the evening, Charchar and Ignacio da Souza arrived with the ostentation, dirt, and display of African officials.

May 24. Crossed the swamp; rather bad. Arrived at Zobardoh, and put up in a neat farm-house in a fine cultivated country.

May 25. Arrived at Canamina. This being the same route I took in my last mission, I do not describe it. Cana deserves a line in praise. The level park-lands, the high state of cultivation, neatness and cleanliness of habitation, aged of both sexes, sereneness of atmosphere—all combined, lead the ideas far from Africa, slavery, and sacrifices. Dahomey, carrying war and devastation into all the neighbouring countries, has herself enjoyed the sweets of peace. It is not the Dahomians who war, but forced mercenaries; nor are the Dahomians much the gainers by these harassing slave-hunts—old age is decapitated to ornament the Palace, strength and youth sold to enrich the Brazils, their proceeds wasted at the horrible and ridiculous Customs of "Hivae noo ee wha", occurring once a year. Charchar arrived. Sent to Abomey to report our arrival; received in answer that we rise at cock-crow and proceed.

May 26. At 7 arrived at Abomey. Immediately inside the gate, on wheels (a present from the late Charchar), was a brigantine about twenty-eight feet long, well rigged, under all plain sail, union-jack at the fore, French tricolour at the peak. Dressed in full uniform, Charchar and Brazilians arrived and took guard ahead of us, attended by 140 armed slaves in Dahomian uniforms. At 9 we were met by the Cabooceers. I have described a meeting before. The Charchar was bent on giving us his left, in which he failed; and to show his bad taste, muttered audibly "Politico, politico!" A messenger arriving from the King addressed him, in hopes that he and his "whites" were quite well; he was constrained to pass on to us and thus showed we were two parties. It is somewhat odd that the late Da Souza was the patron of nearly all English visitors to Abomey, Mr Duncan, Dr Dickson, and nearly so to Mr Cruickshanks. Forming procession, the Cabooceers preceded them, Mr Beecroft and myself followed by the Charchar, the guns of the saluting battery firing twenty-one guns in honour of Her Majesty Queen Victoria, and thirteen each for Her Majesty's Plenipotentiaries.

The King's reception was much the same as described in my former mission—we were received first, and the Charchar "passed" first; honours were divided. The court-yard was decorated with flags of all colours; among them many union-jacks, intended doubtless as a compliment, although the only other great display was of human skulls. I remarked last journal, that the skull-ornaments of the wall were in many parts blown down; now there are few left, and the King has no intention of renewing them. Yet how inconsistent! the Palaver-house, in the centre of the square, was ornamented with 148 newly cleaned from the Okeadon war (one of the most cowardly acts that ever disgraced a tyrant). The only other ornament was a gaudy tent in front of the Palace, under which was a State chair. At noon we were permitted to retire to our new home in the Mayo's Palace, having taken a mixture—in the United States called "stone wall"—of rum, gin, brandy, beer, hock, lemonade gazeuse, besides liqueurs. In the evening the Mayo visited.

May 27. The Mayo visited, and invited us to be present at his levee (assembly, reception).

The Palace of Dangelahcordeh has many gates; to-day at each gate a Minister held his levee. At 2 PM we arrived at the Mayo's, whose canopy of umbrellas formed the apex from which a ring was extended, here and there studded with umbrellas and banners; on a high stool of state sat the Minister, surrounded by his officers, who left a lane in front for new-comers to advance through and salute the chief. On our arrival we were seated on his right, and exchanged compliments in a glass of Frontignac. In the ring were two bands, and in gaudy attire two troubadours (the only appropriate names for them; they were not minstrels, and certainly not ballad-singers, but between the two); each carried a staff of office—a blue crutch stick with a device carved in the staff, and to each stick was a yellow handker-chief. They sang about the wars of the Dahomians and histories of the Kings of Dahomey; in this way only are the records kept. The troubadours were father and son, and the office is hereditary and lucrative; if failing male heir, by adoption.

About an hour after our arrival, headed by guards, ban-ners, and official emblems, arrived His Majesty's sisters and daughters, followed by bands of discordant music and attendants carrying changes of raiment, gaudily dressed in cotton cloths and coral and Popo beads. The Princesses, about thirty in number, took possession on our right in front, and made it very warm. The elder troubadour was soon dismissed, the younger pleased better. After remaining about an hour, the royal ladies rose *en masse*, and each pro-ducing a small decanter, which it appeared was her prerog-ative to have filled with rum, assailed the aged Minister. A scene followed, highly derogatory to the dignity of royalty. As soon as all were satisfied, they took leave, and forming procession marched off to the next gate, where a similar scene followed. During this time the Mayo received his friends, and entertained each with a glass before he dismissed him; all knelt when approaching him and threw dirt on their heads. Taking leave, we called in at the Viceroy's levee; who regaled us with beer and effervescing lemonade. These levees are called *Zandro*.

May 28. At 8 AM, in full uniform, we were commanded to the Palace, and according to the Court etiquette, were gazed at by the many-headed for an hour. During the Customs, each Minister, Cabooceer, or military officer, has to assemble his men at 6, and when dressed and ready (every morning), to make the circuit of the Palace Square in procession three times. At the arrival at the gate in each round, he has to prostrate, while his retainers fire, dance, and sing; this finished, if on duty, he places his insignia of office under a long tent, and stretches himself on a mat until required: if not, he plants his umbrella, and, seated on his stool, holds a short levee, and then retires. At 9 we entered the Palace, and were shown to the entrée of the audience-chamber; His Majesty lounged on a bed. There were present the Mayo, Yavogau, Cambodee, Toonoonoo, and Maehaepah—Minister of Foreign Affairs, Viceroy of Whydah, Treasurer, Head-Eunuch, and the Amazon Grand Vizier. The seal of Her Majesty's letter having been broken by the King, Mr Beecroft read it in short sentences to the interpreters (three, and unfortunately none of the best).

As far as could be judged, His Majesty received its contents with pleasure; promised to consider the question; directed us to view his Customs well.

From certain remarks elucidated concerning the emoluments [profits] of the Slave Trade, we considered it prudent to acquaint His Majesty that we were authorized to offer a subsidy, and we were in power to put it in force immediately His Majesty should enter into a treaty; but that

it was impossible to pronounce the sum until we had witnessed his disbursements.

The interview was flattering. On our return, sent the
Queen's gracious presents.

The Ministers and Cabooceers paraded the town at the
head of their bands and retainers, firing constantly.

May 29. At 7.30 we were again ushered into the audience
entrée, now occupied by Maehaepah, very busy winding
up, one after another, eight Sam Slick's clocks, some upside-
down, others on their sides, and one, by mistake, in its proper
position; from this state we rescued them, but not before I
had horrified the stately dame by placing one foot within
the sacred precincts of the harem. To prevent so unprece-
dented an occurrence, the Maehaepah and Toonoonoo
knelt one on each side the threshold, and thus exhibited
clocks, musical-boxes, watches, etc. on the particular effica-
cies of each of which we were called upon to dilate.

At 10 we passed through another gate. Entering a large
court-yard, on the opposite side, under a canopy of umbrellas of every colour, and ornamented with strange devices,
sat the King on a sofa, and over him a small European para-
sol of crimson-velvet and gold. His Majesty wore a blue
flowered satin robe, a gold-laced hat, and sandals ornamented with silver; round his neck a neat gold chain.

On the side of the court occupied by the throne sat the
royal wives and female officers, all well-dressed in a varie-
gation of silks, cloths, etc. and the Amazons in full uniform,
all seated on their hams, rested the stocks of their long
Danish muskets on the ground, while the polished barrels
stook up like a forest. In one part of the female group sat
twenty-eight with blue crutch sticks, each ornamented
with a yellow handkerchief; these were the sticks of office
of the female troubadours, and each was to relate in her
own way the romance of history of Dahomey.

Standing facing the throne (the Mayo, Yavogau, and Cabooceer of the British Fort, Heechelee, lay prostrated, throwing dirt on their heads), we bowed three times to the King. This was a neutral ground, and was occupied during the day by the Maehaepah and Toonoonoo, or the female Grand Vizier and Head Eunuch, who, on their knees, communicated the royal pleasure or any message. The King, being guarded by his Amazons, could not be approached by one of the opposite sex. On this neutral ground were the skulls of Kings in calabashes [gourds] surrounding a newly turned heap, which contained the head of a victim sacrificed last night, his body to be buried under the tent (pole) to be used by His Majesty to-morrow. Some of these skulls were ornamented with brass, copper, coral, etc.: one in a copper pan illustrated a fearful tale of treachery and murder, the skull of Ahchardee, Chief of Jena.

After saluting the Monarch we turned round, and on the opposite side were from 300 to 400 males, Ministers, Cabooceers, officers and soldiers. As with the Amazons, in one part were twenty-eight sticks belonging to troubadours; all were shaded by large umbrellas. Immediately opposite the throne were chairs and a table set with decanters and glasses for ourselves, under a canopy of handsome umbrellas; on the right sat the Charchar and the Brazilians, similarly accommodated.

Taking our seats, the *coup-d'œil* was very pleasing: all were well-dressed; the Ministers and Cabooceers in flowing robes. Besides the diversity of colour in dress and umbrellas, there were also number of banners and Fetish ornaments. The day's jubilee is named "Eh nah ek begh" (the Day of Giving).

Business commenced by two male troubadours introducing themselves; then one at a time recited the exaggerated accounts of the wild warlike adventures of Guezo and his ancestors; interlucent praises and visionary accounts of the future. As though gratifying to the Monarch who had deposed him, they desecrated the name of his brother Adonooza, as totally unfit to reign over a powerful and brave nation such as the Dahomian. At the mention of the name of any member of the Royal Family deceased, all the Ministers, Cabooceers, and officers, male and female, had to prostrate and kiss the dust, etc. The troubadours by no means spared them: they hailed Guezo as the greatest of African Monarchs; he had only to command, and it was done; enumerated all the conquered States. That any country that insulted Dahomey must fall; and there still remained three to conquer, Tappah, Yoruba, and Abbeokuta. Two Amazons next spouted their visionary lore, amusing themselves at times calling on the multitude to laugh for joy at the recital of the King's exploits: when first, the females would exercise their risible faculties, then the males give a sort of Irish howl; now and again the singers called on the multitude to join chorus, which was readily complied with. As each two were attended by a discordant band, there was no lack of music.

At 3 PM, raining hard, we were commanded to retire.

Seated five hours over damp ground. Had it not been for the novelty, would, doubtless, have been irksome.

In the evening the Mayo, Yavogau, and Narwhey, attended by the Royal command to explain to us the expenses of the day, and brought strings of cowries, which we had to count, to satisfy ourselves of the correctness of their statement.

Before leaving, the Mayo solemnly charged us, that neither ourselves nor our servants be found in the streets to-night; His Majesty was going to sacrifice to the manes of his ancestors.

May 30. At 7.30 we started for the Palace. At a little distance from our house, the road was fenced off; the King's wives were going to carry goods to market, and no one might meet them.

At the foot of the ladder ascending to the Palaver-House, in the square of the Palace of Dangelahcordeh, lay six newly-cut-off human heads, the blood still oozing; at the threshold of the entrance gate was a pool of human blood. Within, the scene was entirely different from yesterday: in the centre of the Palace-court stood a huge crimson cloth tent, forty feet high, and of forty feet diameter, ornamented with devices of men cutting off others' heads, calabashes full of human heads, and other emblems of brutality and barbarity; on the top stood the figure of a Dahomian, with half his head shaved, supporting a staff from which flew a white standard; on it was emblazoned a jar, having one skull for a stopper, standing in a large dish on three other skulls (blue). Although the King had not arrived, we had to pay the same compliment as yesterday (similarly attended) to the throne, which was inside the tent, around which were the Amazons, wives, etc. On the neutral ground were the same skulls. Turning round, our position faced His Majesty's, and about were the Ministers, etc. all dressed as near as possible alike, in red striped flowing robes, and laden with necklaces. In a short time His Majesty arrived, dressed in a coloured silk robe and laced hat. Having taken his seat on the throne under the tent, the business of the day commenced by a procession of fifty-eight Ministers and Cabooceers, each carrying a sword, a scimitar, and a club. After passing the throne three times, all prostrated, and threw dirt on their heads.

To give the whole account would be to make this journal prolix [lengthy]; the processions lasted till 3 PM, and comprised between 6,000 and 7,000 people. I here shall merely make a few comments.

The day's Custom is called "Ek bah tong ek beh" (Carrying Goods to Market), and is really a display of as much of the whole wealth of the Monarch as can be, without material damage, drawn or carried to the market of Ahjahhee and back; a distance, both ways, of about a mile. The day was cloudy, and the dresses by no means good. From the programme a very fair calculation of the actual wealth of the King may be made: 1,793 women carried cowries, each three heads, on an average, some not more than half-a-head; being in total 5,379 heads of cowries or dollars. Among the display of wealth were many articles of little value—some 50 pots-de-chambre, to wit—His Majesty could not be aware of the use of; 90 women carried common jugs; 170 carried each one piece of cloth cut in two and rolled; 46 ditto white baft ditto; 47 carried each six Dutch pipes; 70 ditto empty blue bottles; 50 carried a washing-jug each. It has been frequently related to me, that His Majesty possesses whole services of plate. How ridiculous! The collection of a country fair, carried in a similar manner, would have far exceeded the wealth displayed in value and appearance. The dresses of a minor theatre would have excelled.

In a country like Dahomey it is an immense collection, but when the exactions of the Monarch are considered, scarcely to be wondered at. If a Dahomian receives a present he must lay if before the King, and if admired, even the Prime Minister would find it more to his interest to forego it.

Besides goods carried, there were several bands of troops, male and female, and several tasteful groups at different periods took position, danced and sang before the King. Bands were playing in all directions; dwarfs, hunchbacks, court fools, albinos, besides an ostrich and an emu, and several dogs of strange breed strolled about the neutral ground; lastly came the ancient ladies, and those holding offices of regal rank, with the insignia of their separate offices; among them numbers of human skulls in drums, banners, knives, etc. These were disgusting enough, but to behold twelve unfortunate human victims for to-morrow's sacrifice—carried round, eight on men's, four on women's heads, bound hand and foot and tied in small canoes, dressed in white with high glazed red caps, followed by an alligator and a cat, also for sacrifices—was fearfully so. As the victims passed the throne of their superstitious tyrant they were halted, and addressed by the Mayo on the munificence of the Monarch, who sent them each a head of cowries wherewith to purchase a last meal.

Once during the day the King left his tent to pay us a visit and drink a glass of liqueur.

As yesterday, the Maehaepah and Toonoonoo were continually engaged, and each point of the proceedings was explained to us through this channel from His Majesty.

At 3 it rained hard, and we were allowed to leave, with much to reflect upon.

Rum was distributed in bottles to the different companies, and about 800 dollars in cowries.

May 31. At 7 AM we were summoned to witness the Custom called "Ek gaee noo Ahtoh" (Throwing away Cowries from Ahtoh).

As we left our house His Majesty was passing, and sent us a bottle of rum. Joining in procession we were followed by the Amazon host. Passing round the walls of the Palace of Dangehlahcordeh we arrived on an open ground called Ahjahhee, at once the market-place and parade-ground, and now occupied by a huge raised platform, hung with cloths and ornamented with banners of every hue, among them two union-jacks, and surmounted by huge umbrellas and small tents. On the west side of this platform or Ahtoh was a fence-work of prickly acacia, outside of which was a band of soldiers; inside fourteen human beings for sacrifice. As soon as the King arrived he ascended the Ahtoh, and immediately several bands of naked men (unless a grass cloth bag round the waist be termed clothing) marched past; in each band several rode on the shoulders of others; headmen; these were the soldiers of the Kings, his sons, the Ministers and Cabooceers.

I believe it has hitherto been supposed that on this particular day of the Customs, His Majesty enjoys a species of liberality unknown in the annals of the histories of any other known nations, in the scrambling to his people goods of all descriptions—cowries, silk, tobacco, rum, etc., and also live sacrifices. I say I believe so, for such has been my own opinion, deduced from Dalyell and from report. Such is by no means the case. The public are not admitted to the scramble, and the whole performance is a cheat. The scramblers, as has been stated, are the soldiers (about 300), and the goods are their pay, and this day did not amount to more than 1,000 dollars in cowries and 300 dollars in cloth. The throwing away occupied between seven and eight hours.

Taking seats on the left, the King (all being hustled together) addressed the scramblers, directing them not to fight or quarrel, and having thrown a few by way of trial, commanded us into his presence. Ascending the Ahtoh, the scene was extraordinary: the floor was laid with rushes, and on it about 3,000 heads of cowries, and 500 pieces of cloth, besides rum and tobacco; at one end, under a gorgeous umbrella, dressed in a black waistcoat, a cotton cloth round his loins, and a white nightcap, stood the King, labouring hard "throwing goods". Under a range of umbrellas, facing the multitude, stood the Ministers and Cabooceers, one of which remained vacant for our use. The back part of the Ahtoh was occupied by small tents for the ladies of the Harem; while, as we entered, under separate canopies, were two tables set with decanters, etc. for ourselves and the Charchar to retire to.

Taking our stand under the umbrella, the crowd appeared to be one living mass of humanity. Cowries became the property of the lucky ones who caught them: but not so the cloths—no sooner caught, than if not handed to the headmen riders, a fight ensued terrible to behold, the riders running over the mob as if on dry land, and it was sure to be found.

As the mass oscillated, it emitted an effluvium only to be compared to the fetid vapour that rises from the over-crowded decks of a slave-ship, and a steam arose as dense as the miasm from a swamp. A guard of soldiers paraded the area during the day.

Soon after our arrival, His Majesty sent us a present of ten heads of cowries and two pieces of cloth.

During the day, several presents were given, altogether to the amount of 1,000 heads of cowries, and about 200 pieces of cloth, a little rum and tobacco. Among the recipients were two Kings, an Ashantee ambassador, a head mallum, etc.

About noon the brigantine before alluded to was drawn up, and a lane made through the mob; a boat on wheels put off to land her cargo of rum, cloth, and cowries, etc. At 10 we breakfasted, supplied by His Majesty, and after breakfast joined the King in "throwing away". It was easy to observe that one party was the grand receiver, and that party the King's. Acting on this, a man named Pohvehsoo, captain of musketoons and court fool, and as we have since heard, headsman, had ingratiated himself; knowing him to be the King's friend, we aimed three cloths filled with cowries at him; having received the third, His Majesty ordered him off, as having had enough.

If I were to conclude the history of this day's Customs here, I should merely remark that there might be a policy in making appear munificence the distribution of a sum of money, that if doled out to each individually, would prove a miserable pittance, although it tended much to debase the minds of his people, if that were possible. But what follows is almost too revolting to be recorded.

As if by general consent, and evincing a slight dawning of decency, hardly to be expected from these truly barbarians, silence reigned, and when broken, the eunuchs would strike a metal instrument each was supplied with, to enforce it, sounding the knell of eleven unfortunate human beings, whose only crime known to their persecutors was that they belonged to a nation Dahomey had warred against, Attahpam. Out of fourteen now brought upon the platform, we, the unworthy instruments of Providence, succeeded in saving the lives of three. Lashed as described in yesterday's journal, except that only four were in boats, the remainder in baskets, these unfortunates, gagged, met the gaze of their enemies with a firmness perfectly astonishing—not a sigh was breathed. One cowardly villain put his hands to the eyes of a victim, who sat with his head down, to feel for moisture; finding none, he drew upon himself the ridicule of his hellish coadjutors.

Ten of these human offerings to the vitiated appetite of his soldiers, and the alligator and cat, were guarded by the male soldiers, and to the right of the King; four to the left were guarded by women.

Being commanded into the presence, the King asked if we wished to be present at the sacrifice; with horror we declined, and begged to be allowed to save a few by purchasing. After a little hesitation, we were asked which we would have; I claimed the first and last of the ten, while Mr Beecroft claimed the nearest of the four, and 100 dollars being stated as the price, was gladly accepted. In all my life I never saw such coolness so near death: the most attentive ear could not have caught the breath of a sigh—it did not look reality, yet it soon proved fearfully so.

Retiring to our seats, the King insisted on our viewing the place of sacrifice. Immediately under the Royal canopy were six or eight executioners, armed with large knives, grinning horribly; the mob now armed with clubs and branches, yelled furiously, calling upon the King to "feed them—they were hungry".

Scarcely had we reached our seats, when a demoniac yelling caused us to look back. The King was showing the immolations to his people, and now they were raised high over the heads of their carriers, while the Monarch made a speech to the soldiers, telling them that these were of the prisoners from Attahpam; he called their names. The Charchar left at the same time with ourselves; but Ignacio and Antonio da Souza remained spectators.

The unfortunate being nearest the King, stripped of his clothes, was now placed on end on the parapet, the King giving the upper part of the boat an impetus, a descent of twelve feet stunned the victim, and before animation could return, the head was off; the body, beaten by the mob, was dragged by the heels to a pit at a little distance, and there left a prey to wolves and vultures.

After the third the King retired; not so the slave-merchants. When all was over, at 3 PM, we were permitted to retire. At the foot of the ladder in the boats and baskets lay the bleeding heads. It is my duty to describe; I leave exposition to the reader.

June 1. At noon we sallied forth to witness a novel sight; a review, half males, half Amazons. The Custom is called "Eh dah sol ek begh" (Firing Guns). The parade-ground in the Ahjahhee market-place was now clear, the Ahtoh had disappeared, and all that remained to mark the fearful tragedy of yesterday were the stains of blood, emitting a pestilential stench.

Having taken our seats under some shady trees, the troops marched past in the following order. First came the Cabooceers and their retainers, some 300; lastly, the King's levees, and those of the Royal Family, in all 4,400 men; then came the Amazons in the same order, 2,400. In each regiment or company, first came the armed, then the banners, stool of office, followed by the officers under umbrellas; lastly, the band. In the rear of each of the King's levees, male and female, was an equal number of stools, banners, drums, and umbrellas, all ornamented with skulls and jawbones.

At 12.30 His Majesty arrived, and took his seat on a high stool under a canopy of umbrellas. On his left the Charchar; on his right Mr Beecroft and myself. Under the canopy were none but males. Toonoonoo remained outside, and Maehaepah hovered in the neighbourhood, ready to communicate, if required.

The King must be aware of the consequences of too often raising the evil passions of men, and too long indulging his people with murder. As if by the power of Aladdin's lamp, to-day they were a changed nation, totally military; the King was a soldier, in French grey tunic, short trousers, and fur skull-cap; no sandals, and no ornaments except a neat cartouche-box and other military apparel. The hunchback and dwarf vied with the court-fool in military address; in all this there was nothing very extraordinary; but when, in the midst of the Amazons stood the royal mother, wives, female Ministers, all in uniform, and armed each with a musket, sword, and club, and which each showed she knew well how to use, the Monarch looked to us, as if to say, "Did you ever witness the like of this?" All were well, and many handsomely, uniformly, dressed.

The whole marched past a second and a third time. Seventy-seven banners and 160 huge umbrellas flirted by the bearers, muskets ornamented with ribbons, flying aloft to be caught again, together enlivening the scene; while 55 discordant bands, and the shouts of soldiery as they hailed the Monarch, almost deafened the observer.

The retainers of the Ministers and Cabooceers now occupied the ground at the farther end of the field, when first the royal male levees (headed by an emblem of a leopard killing a snake, on a staff) advanced, skirmishing to the foot of the throne, keeping up a constant fire. In front was a regiment of blunderbuss-men, bush-rangers in green grass surtouts. Halting in front, they gave the salute, holding up their muskets with their right hands, their left rattling a small metal rattle each soldier wears round the neck; while some, having light pieces, flung them aloft to catch them again; all the officers prostrating, and throwing dirt on their heads.

The King rose and left the canopy, said one or two words to them, and receiving a light musket from an aide-de-camp, fired it, and received one of many now offered. He then danced a war-dance. It commenced with a quick-step march; presently he halted, and putting his hand over his eyes, scanned the distance, sent out scouts; danced again, again halted; now certain the enemy was in sight, fired his piece. The soldiers shouted, fired, advanced, and retired, and the King returned to his seat, shaking hands with us, telling us he had been to war.

At 6.30 the review ended, and we were permitted to retire, much pleased with the day's amusement. During the whole proceedings, order and discipline were observable; the uniformity of dress exceedingly striking. The show of colours, variety of the flat-topped umbrellas, various devices and emblems like the eagles of the Romans, the highly-polished muskets—all combined, the effect was as pleasing as it was novel.

I am now accustomed to skulls, but a sense of disgust arose when the King sent the Meigau's drinking (war) cup for our inspection—it was a polished human skull. The

Meigau, the highest officer in the realm, holds, among other offices, that of hereditary headsman—under a Dahomian Monarch, no sinecure, although he has a band of subordinates.

The 6,800 soldiers reviewed, with perhaps an equal number on the frontiers, form the standing army of Dahomey; certainly not more than 14,000 male and female, and nearly all foreigners, bought or prisoners of war. When the King makes war, he levies, according to its capabilities, from each town and district; but, I should say, never marched more than 20,000 to war, leaving about 8,000 armed men under the Mayo to protect his capital and frontiers.

I do not think His Majesty gave us credit for being able to count his troops, but we had done so before he arrived on the ground; and luckily we had, for afterwards several of the largest regiments would march past twice, and one of them three times, thus swelling out the apparent numbers.

During the day he appeared anxious we should have every information, and frequently sent the names of the chiefs as they passed.

June 3. Again the Custom called "Ek bah tong ek begh", and preceded as before by six human sacrifices, which lay in two heaps under the steps of the Palaver-House, as we passed into the court of the Palace of Dangelahcordeh at 7.30 AM.

The day was fine, and dresses beautiful in appearance; the tent and positions the same. The opening scene—the procession of Ministers and Cabooceers—was as splendid as it could have been; all wore crimson and yellow slashed silk robes, and over these the Ministers wore crimson silk-velvet cloaks trimmed with gold.

Among the groups the most showy were the six Paussee ladies; one wore a Charles II hat and milk-white plume; the other five wore gilt helmets with red and green plumes, tunics of scarlet and gold, with bands of green satin, and waist-belts of blue and green silk; coral bead necklaces, silver gauntlets and armlets, attended by 200 Amazons under arms in scarlet tunics; also a group of six ex-ladies of the Royal Chamber, all mothers of the King, and his present favourite wife, in tunics of country cloth, and similarly ornamented as above, except that each wore at her girdle a polished human skull-cap, and each wore a white slouched hat trimmed with gold-lace. The scene was much more brilliant than on the last day.

Let it be remembered that these Customs occur only once a year, and have been annually for 100 years; and that many of the dresses (which are worn on no other occasion) are much older. I had almost forgotten to mention that these dresses did not save the eternal prostration.

Before going away, His Majesty invited us into his tent, to the too well expressed astonishment of 200 ladies, who must have thought the King had parted with his senses when he admitted men and strangers into their sanctuaries. His Majesty proved himself to be sane, by telling us that to-morrow he wished us to measure the tent, and put down in our note-books that he wanted two, and two sofas.

Inside, the tent was supported like an umbrella, and apparently very old; in the centre was the sofa, and over it a white umbrella; on the sofa were child's toys.

At 5.30 we left, having sat too long over damp ground. At 7 we were again commanded to attend the King to an evening Custom, "El doo beh pah meh," "Go to pah meh" (To Eat). His Majesty went in procession, attended by all the Ministers, wives, Cabooceers, and both armies.

Arrived at the market, some edibles were brought to us; but as it was very dark, we did not eat of them. The King was said to be throwing away eatables to the people; we did not see or hear it. His Majesty sent us four heads of cowries each, and permitting us to depart, we reached home at 10.

June 6. Most of the town was closed to-day, as the ladies of the royal harem went forth to bathe.

June 9. *Sunday*. The Charchar, his brothers, and Domingo, have been closeted all day with the King. The late Da Souza's debts are said to be the palaver.

June 10. At five miles north-west of Abomey is a beautiful view, which we visited this morning. Leaving the town, the ground gradually rises until suddenly the road opens on a deep extensive valley of undulating ground. Far as the eye can see are the Dabadab Mountains, looking blue in the distance; our eye having been so constantly accustomed to level views, looked upon this as magnificent, and the keen air blowing clear from such a distance, gave us an excellent appetite for a picnic breakfast. On the upper ground was clay with ironstone, sandstone, conglomerate, and chalk. Descending into this valley, a walk of a mile and a half brought us to a swamp of discoloured water, the only watering-place of Abomey, and from hence the water is carried on the heads of women. In the valley the soil is oozy and fertile; but unfortunately, except here and there, miles apart, there are no habitations.

In the evening, Domingo Jozé Martins, the greatest slave-dealer in all Africa, called to take leave. He remained upwards of an hour; and, in conversation, told us that last year, by palm-oil alone, he cleared 70,000 dollars, and shipped in one month from Porto Novo, 300 tons of oil, or 10 tons a-day. In conversing about the Slave Trade, he said the only thing that supported it was its being contraband. In speaking of his individual position, the monopoly of Porto Novo, that one trade helped the other.

June 11. As an introduction to the day's proceedings (the commencement of the War Palaver), it is necessary to give some account of the present state of the Dahomian army, which is at once divided into two divisions, the right and the left, the advanced and the rear, or the Meigau's and the Mayo's, or the general's titles, the Agaou's and the Passoo's. In each of these two divisions is a battalion of males, and one of Amazons.

The army has another extraordinary division—the male and the Amazon. In each army is a Meigau, a Mayo, an Agaou, a Passoo; and each male officer or soldier has his equivalent in rank in the Amazon lines, termed "Mother". The Meigau's levees are 140, the Mayo's 300, etc.; those of their coadjutors are equally numbered, or nearly so. The Charchar and all visitors have "mothers" also. Our "mother", the Yawae, is a most distinguished soldier.

Their pay is precarious; clothed and fed; armed and supplied with powder; as will be seen, they swear to conquer or die. Prisoners and heads are purchased from the captors, and the reward at the Customs depends on the success in the war.

In or about 1625, Tahcohdohnoh, King of Tahhee, marched upon a small town (now called Abomey), and accomplished a vow to the Fetish by ripping open the belly of the captured Prince, and placing his body under the foundation of a new palace, which he appropriately called "Dahomey", or Dah's belly: hence the name also of the Kingdom of Dahomey.

At 10 AM we entered the Palace of Dahomey at a gate called "Ah goh doh meh". The King reclined under a canopy in a low shed-like building: the positions were similar to those described on previous days. In our rear were the mausoleums of Kings—small thatched round houses, each surmounted by a silver ornament of large size; in front of each was a heap of human skulls and bones, and at the door of each a pillar of cloth shaded by an umbrella. On the neutral ground were strewed cooked meats, etc., and hundreds of turkey buzzards flew about with sickening familiarity.

The Custom called "Seh que ah ee" (Watering the Graves) is in honour of Tahcohdohnoh and his successors.

Singing had commenced; and shortly after, from the tenor of the song, a dispute arose which became a war palaver.

At 3 we left. Before breaking up, four human beings were sacrificed (decapitated). The cowries distributed did not exceed 30 dollars (heads).

June 12. A respectable liberated African woman called to say that her husband, also from Sierra Leone, was a prisoner of war. Her story is as follows: ten years since they came to Whydah. Her husband has been much subject to the hooping-cough, and hearing of a doctor (native) in Attapham, went there. War came, and both he and the doctor were taken prisoners. We promised to intercede. His name is John McCarthy.

June 13. At noon I arrived at the parade-ground. Mr Beecroft unwell. His Majesty occupied a similar position to that of June 1, and I joined him under his canopy: on his right, under canopies of umbrellas, were the principal ladies and Amazon generals, etc.; scattered over the field were the different regiments of Amazons, one had passed and another was advancing to the foot of the throne. The custom was the Amazons swearing to be faithful next war. In these swearings it is customary to ask for a particular place for attack, and if asked for three times it is generally granted. Bah or Abbeokuta has been asked for twice; first the King went to Kangaroo, then made a feint, and fell upon Okeadon; now they ask confidently. The language was constantly in parables and metaphors, continually a crier hailed the King as "Ah hau soo lae hee Hausso": Oh! King of Kings.

The regiment now before the King was of bushrangers, with three stripes of whitewash round each leg; they first saluted their officers, then the King, when one after another three stepped forward and swore in the name of the regiment to conquer or die.

The King's own regiment then advance and deposit their Fetish in front (about 300). They are joined by about 200 women belonging to the late Charchar, who state they are young soldiers and are come to witness the review. All sing (to the King), "You alone on earth we will serve."

The colonel advances and prostrates, then says, "The Attahpams wanted strength to fight against Guezo. Let us go to Bah, and if we do not conquer, our heads are at your disposal. They will run: if into water we can follow; if into fire or up trees, we can catch them."

Another regiment, attended by the present Charchar's head wife, ornamented with much gold, advance. They salute me and beg me to convey their thanks to Her Majesty for 2,000 caps sent them by Cruickshanks. Wherever they wear them there they will be victorious.

All 2,000 Amazons assemble in front of the throne. "If beans be dried in the fire, cannot one put her fingers in to take out to eat. (All sing.) When we went to Attahpam we found nobody; all ran away; if they reached the water (sea) they will be turned into salt. At Bah let the rear be the advance."

It rained hard, and a mat was sloped over the King and myself; still the Amazons kept their ground, and as they were not likely otherwise to be heard, several danced, while all sang, after which they swear again.

A girl six years old came forward and said, "The King opened his mouth three times when he spoke of war, once now will be sufficient; let that once be on Bah."

All call on Souza to act like his father, and get plenty of ships for the King. "When the porcupine sheds a quill, another takes its place." All prostrate, and throw dirt, while criers call the King's names. He receives a new one for the

Attahpam war, of "Hausso Ghah Glah", King of Chimpanzees, that drives men from their farms.

An Amazon: As the blacksmith takes an iron bar and fashions it, so have we changed our nature: we are men. We have powder, and the King has promised to tell the Agaou the intended seat of war; we have been waiting long; let us lead at once to Bah. The King gives us cloth, but thread is required to make the garments; we are the thread. Corn put out to dry should be looked to, or the goats will eat. Look to Bah, lest like the Attahpams they remove all their treasure. A cask of rum cannot roll itself. A table in a house becomes useful when anything is placed on it. The Dahomian army without the Amazons are as both.

Another: If one does not spit, the belly is uneasy; if the hand be not outstretched, it receives nothing.

All the officers stand in front; all the Amazons raise their muskets and shout "Soh jae mee" (May thunder kill us if we break our oaths). They hail the King as Koparsalmee (the eagle). As he leaves the canopy, all prostrate, and rise as His Majesty receives an ebony club. He then addresses them, "If a hunter buys a dog and trains him, he takes him unto the forest without telling him his errand; if he sees a beast he sends the dog after it; should the dog return without the game, the hunter kills him and leaves his carcase to the turkey buzzards. If I tell my daughters to put their fingers in the fire, they must obey; if I order you to clear the bush and you do not do it, what will I do to you? Do you think I will not punish you? If you are taken prisoners you know your fate. Your heads become ornaments and your bodies feed the wolves and vultures. Where you are sent there you must fight."

King dances and drinks; then hands round rum in a tin dish. Amazons drink. He returns to the tent, and all march off.

June 20. The captains of Charchar's troops told one of our interpreters to tell us if there were any whites in Abbeokuta, we had better warn them, as the King intended to make war on Abbeokuta.

June 22. At 10.30 entered the Palace of Dangelahcordeh at the King's mother's gate, called Ahcontehneh. The position much the same as before. At the gate was a similar oven similarly ornamented. Under two umbrellas, to the left of the King, sat the Ahcontehneh, and one lady handsomely dressed. First passed a number of Amazons, band of music playing, and receiving a few heads of cowries; then the Amazon officers advanced and saluted the King. Sing. Called upon all eyes to behold the glory of Guezo, there are not two but one, one only in the world—Guezo. Every nation has its Customs, but none so brilliant or enlightened as Dahomey. See, all nations send their ambassadors, black and white.

> *Chorus*: Look round and behold
> Ambassadors of all nations.

All officers, male and female, prostrate and throw dirt.

All Amazon officers sing. "Yorubas lied when they said we could not conquer them. When we meet we will make their day as night. Let the rain fall quickly, that the river may be dried soon. Yoruba and Dahomey cannot drink out of the same glass; two rams cannot drink out of the same calabash. The Yorubas must have been drunk when they said they would conquer Dahomey."

An Amazon: In days gone by, the white trader brought good articles; they do not do so now. Then a musket lasted twenty years; it now lasts three.

Deputation of public women.

Toonoonoo: You have sung sweetly; sing more.

All Amazons sing: "There's a difference between the King and a poor man. There's a difference between the King and a rich man. Let a man be ever so rich, and Guezo is still King over him. All guns are not cast alike: some are long, some are short. If men are drunk they are not fit to live. There is a nation that must fall: Abbeokuta. Thus we will dance before all." (Dance.)

Criers cry the King's names, and say there is a leaf called Eeaboo*: let the King cause a Fetish to be made with it, and Bah must fall. Everything Guezo does is well done. His power is supreme over the male and female of all kinds.

Mahtohseh, Fetish chief, addressing the Amazon officers: "Your songs have been pleasing, you cannot do better than sing again."

All Amazons sing: "With these guns in our hands and powder in our cartouche-boxes, what has the King to fear? When we go to war, let the King dance, while we bring him prisoners."

One Amazon officer calls the King's sons and sings to them: "Pray to Seh (God) that your father's days may be long in the land. Let all the King's family pray to their ancestors for long life to Guezo. If a leopard kills her prey, does she not feed her young first? If a deer bears young, does she not chop the grass for it?"

Bondohhoo, the King's eldest son: "All the days of my life I shall pray for longer life for my father."

All officers of both sexes salute the King.

July 1. Mayo called to inform us he was going to the King to ask him to appoint a day for a palaver. In the evening he returned and informed us the King would appoint an early day. We had a long conversation with him about the Treaty.

July 2. Mayo and Yavogau called to give us the King's account of his expenditure during these Customs, first explaining that there were seven more to go through:

*Poison, perhaps.

the cleaning of the ship—dancing and singing at the Dangelahcordeh gate—dinner and firing guns along the road to and from Whydah—war palaver at Coomassee—custom to his father at Ahgongroo—the war—Fetish custom, which last up to the time of the next watering the graves. They brought 16 strings, each containing 2,000 cowries and 26 odd cowries, or the whole expense for everything, 32,000 heads of cowries, or, deducting one-fourth the difference, 26,000 dollars.

This was an exaggeration, but only proves that His Majesty has some idea of the use of note-books. Again a long palaver about the Slave Trade. On leaving they told us they were going to the King to explain to him our conversation.

July 4. At noon (it had rained hard all the morning) we arrived at the Palace, and at 1 PM were ushered into the audience *entrée* before described. There were present the Mayo, Cambodee, Yavogau, Toonoonoo, and Caoupeh, and their coadjutors in the Harem, and also Maehaepah; all slave-dealers of a large scale. Besides there were Madaki, Narwhey, Magelika, and John Richards, interpreters. Narwhey, one of the greatest slave-merchants, *soi-disant* servant of the English Fort, told Madaki in conversation, that he was working against his own interest in explaining matters to us, saying that the Slave Trade was sweet to him; however, a true translation was given both ways by John Richards. After the usual compliments, the King asked us to make our statement, which was as follows:

> We have seen your Customs and know your amount of expenses. Her Majesty the Queen of Great Britain, for the welfare of the human race, is anxious to stop the Trade in Slaves, and knowing you cannot relinquish it without an equivalent, has sent us, her Plenipotentiaries ("Ah Hausso Noo beh", the Queen's mouth), to endeavour to arrange a

Treaty. In the first place we recommend you to cultivate the soil; all the palm-oil and cotton you can produce cannot supply the British trade, and the present duties on vessels employed in legal trade being (if you stop the other) insufficient, we recommend you to raise it one-half. If you have enemies and are induced to war, make a treaty of trade with the chiefs of those countries, and instead of destroying, cause them to be tributary and make your prisoners of war the means of enriching your own country by the cultivation of the soil. Beyond these means of making your country rich and your name everlasting, Her Majesty, for the term of five years, will yearly send you a present.

The Treaty, if entered into, to be subject to ratification, and not to commence until the first instalment was received.

In answer, His Majesty gave us a history of the foreign trade of Dahomey, from its earliest dates, and the continued good feeling that had always existed between his ancestors and the former Kings of Great Britain; that throughout the Dahomians had sold slaves. He continued:

My people are a military people, male and female; my revenue is the proceeds of the sale of prisoners of war. Did you, after you passed the swamp, except in the neighbour-hood of towns, meet any farms? Other nations deal in slaves, but not like me; they keep all the proceeds to them-selves; I give mine to my people. I would wish the ports of Little Popo, Ahguay, Great Popo, Porto Novo, and Lagos, to be forced to stop the Slave Trade, before I could treat. In the meantime, let the port of Whydah be thrown open to my Slave Trade; not to all the merchants there, but to my agents, Charchar, Domingo Jozé Martins, Joaquim Antonio, Ignacio and Antonio da Souza; let the ships belonging to these five pass free.

We explained to him that what he asked was impossible, and the interpreters wishing it to be put down in a letter to the Queen, we gave them the short negative, which the King understood, and said:

> Charchar has given me one ship, Domingo and Joaquim also one each, make a letter to the Queen to grant me a flag and protection for these three.

We explained that such was impossible, and again had to be expressive and say, No.

At this moment the King's countenance was almost blanched, his head down, his right hand rubbed his forehead, while his veins swelled, and in a tremulous voice he added, "Write to the Queen and ask her to direct her men-of-war to allow 'one' ship to pass in my name to the Brazils, to carry a cargo of slaves, and bring back goods for me." Again we answered, No; the removing of one slave would not be allowed if it could be helped.

> If I stop the Slave Trade how can the Meigau, the Mayo, etc., each of whom, and the merchants, Narwhey, Ahjohbee, Queming, etc., who pay me 5,000 dollars annually (considerably exaggerated), duties and presents, afford to pay their Customs? I cannot send my women to cultivate the soil, it would kill them. My people cannot in a short space of time become an agricultural people. War has destroyed all the neighbouring countries, and my people have to go far for food. All my nation—all are soldiers, and the Slave Trade feeds them.

We now explained to him that if he made his prisoners of war cultivate the soil at home instead of selling them to enrich a foreign land, they would soon be rich; and read to him a second time the Articles offered. Finding we could make no impression, we asked him to dictate a letter in answer to Her Majesty's oft-repeated request, telling him that his wishes regarding the flag and free egress from the port of Whydah were impossible to grant. The Mayo explained that if the Slave Trade was stopped, the King must send to the beach for sand to feed the people on. After some dispute he dictated as follows:

Abomey, July 4, 1850

From Guezo, King of Dahomey, to Her Majesty Queen Victoria.
Being desirous that the Slave Trade should be stopped in the minor ports prior to my entering into a Treaty, I have to request that you will endeavour to blockade the slave-ports between Quittah and Lagos, and then I will endeavour to enter into an agreement for the stoppage of the Slave Trade in my own country.

At present my people are a warlike people and unaccustomed to agricultural pursuits; I should not be enabled to keep up my revenue, were I at once to stop the Slave Trade.

I am always desirous of being at peace with Great Britain.

I am anxious that some person should be sent as Governor to the Fort at Whydah; and having known him, should wish for Lieutenant Forbes, R.N.

Some years ago I entrusted two girls and one boy to the care of Mr Freeman; I am anxious they should be returned.

I am anxious that missionaries should settle at Whydah.

GUEZO, *King of Dahomey* X (his mark)

This letter having been read to the King, Mr Beecroft produced a copy of a letter from the Earl of Chichester to Sagbua, Chief of Abbeokuta. We explained to His Majesty it was too evident he was going to war with that people, and that they were friends of the English people, and that English missionaries resided there. The King answered that he intended making war upon Abbeokuta, and Mr Beecroft had better warn the white men to leave. (I am convinced he intends to attack Abbeokuta after these Customs.)

The Mayo declared that the two Kroomen I had seen last visit had not been found.

The next question was concerning the imprisonment of John McCarthy; the King, evidently annoyed at these questions, ordered the Mayo to inquire about him.

Thus ended the palaver; and I am of opinion that future attempts, unless by force, will fail in causing Guezo to give up the Slave Trade, or his pride admitting him to accept a subsidy. What he recommends to be done to other ports, stopping all trade, if enforced at Whydah, and Lagos be destroyed, the Slave Trade in the Bights will be at an end. The King's selfishness does not save his agents. Little Popo is almost a monopoly of the Charchar's; Great Popo is of Joaquim Antonio; Porto Novo an enormous monopoly of Domingo Jozé Martins.

In everything he said he illustrated simply a desire to enrich himself at the expense of his neighbours.

If his trade be stopped his power is done. At the head of a military nation surrounded by enemies, he must have money, and would then treat for any trade.

In a word, nothing but coercive measures will cause Guezo and his Ministers to give up the Slave Trade.

July 5. Mayo, Yavogau, and Caoupeh came to deliver His Majesty's present, which was as follows:

> For Her Majesty's, two pieces of cloth; Mr Beecroft and
> myself, each one girl to wash our clothes, one Cabooceer's
> stool and foot-stool, one piece of cloth, ten heads of
> cowries, one keg of rum; Madaki, four heads of cowries,

one piece of cloth, one bottle of rum; Richards, two heads, one bottle; hammock-men, two heads, one bottle.

After the present, they explained that His Majesty had given at the last war 4,000 muskets to his soldiers, 4,000 to the Agonee people, and 4,000 he had to give to the new war-men, and that he had equipped these 12,000 soldiers (humbug). Asked when we would start, as he wished to salute Her Majesty and ourselves. The wife of John McCarthy being present, the Mayo took her to recognize her husband, promising to produce him.

July 6. At 7 AM, the Mayo, Yavogau, called, and at the same time the battery fired a salute of twenty-one guns in honour of Her Majesty Queen Victoria, and thirteen each to Mr Beecroft and myself. Drank the health of their Majesties of England and Dahomey.

The Mayo told us that John McCarthy would be sent to Whydah as soon as the King gave orders for his release.

I now asked the Yavogau whether, in case Mr Beecroft and myself coming to Whydah, he would be ready to produce the said John McCarthy; he evaded the question, telling me it was a small palaver, and that the man would be sent.

I then addressed both thus: "I am going to England, and shall acquaint Her Majesty that the King of Dahomey holds a British subject prisoner: you know the consequences to your trade." The shock was electrical; and they begged of me not to be angry. I then threw myself into a passion; dashed a book on the table; and told them I should act as I had told them. They looked much disconcerted.

At 10 started *en route* to Whydah. Arrived at Cana. One of the purchased men was so ill he could not walk, and it occupied me two hours to obtain two men to carry him; and then only because I had declared he should be carried in my hammock if I did not succeed. After leaving Cana at 4 PM, a messenger overtook me, and desired me to stop, explaining that Narwhey and a King's messenger were on the road and wished to speak to me. In a short time they joined, with McCarthy and his wife, and a message from the King, saying that he could not keep a British subject in prison. The wife had been stripped and ironed in the condemned cell.

Narwhey hinted that a present would be acceptable to the King, which was sent from Whydah. Arrived at Tooboodoo.

July 7. Crossed the swamp; twelve hours on the road. Arrived at Whybagou.

July 8. This morning, outside our door, was a party of soldiers guarding two dead bodies of Cabooceers. All headmen are buried at Abomey. Besides that the generality of them have their ancestral houses there, it is a more sure report to the King. Arrived at Allahdah.

July 9. Arrived at Whydah, and found Her Majesty's ship "Bonetta" had anchored the day before.

July 11. Embarked in one of Mr Hutton's canoes, with our hammock-men, all others being directly refused by all parties.

Leaving the Fort, a Fetish snake had during the night killed a cat in the kitchen, and had swallowed all but the two hind legs and tail which remained ungorged; a Fetish woman was sent for to remove it.

F. E. FORBES,
Lieutenant, commanding HMS "Bonetta"

Consul Beecroft to Viscount Palmerston (received October 11)
"Bonetta", West Bay, Prince's Island, July 22, 1850
(Extract)
I have the honour to communicate to your Lordship my proceeding since my last, dated the 4th of May.

I sailed from Fernando Po on the 5th, and arrived at Whydah on the 10th, in Her Majesty's steamer "Phœnix", and landed on the 14th of May, accompanied by Commander Forbes. Left with the presents for the King of Dahomey on the 21st, and arrived at Abomey on the 26th, and was graciously received by His Majesty. He told us that he would give us a day's respite to rest after our journey. Our next interview was on the 28th. I handed to the King Her Majesty's letter; he received it very cordially, and pressed it to his forehead, and then handed it to me to read. The conference relative to the Treaty for the suppression of the foreign Slave Trade was postponed until His Majesty's first Custom was over, which would last about six weeks; we then should have witnessed the most extensive and expensive part of his annual Customs.

The presents from Her Majesty's Government were given over next day to the Mayogau, His Majesty's Prime Minister.

After which I was anxious to have a day appointed to confer on this momentous question; after a great deal of procrastination the 4th of July was the day appointed. It commenced with heavy rain, and continued without inter-mission until 1 o'clock; when it partially cleared away; we then set off for the palace. We, of course, were courteously received by His Majesty.

After a few complimentary remarks from the King, relative to our not remaining to see the whole of the annual Customs and so forth, I told him that it would be five or six months ere the whole of his Customs were finally finished; that would be too long to stop; he said yes, he did not wish it. His Majesty then desired us to proceed with our statement. We then laid before him the subsidy that Her Majesty's Government authorized us to offer to His Majesty the King of Dahomey, annually for five years, instead of three, subject to ratification.

His Majesty made no reply, he was silent on the matter; he did not once refer to the amount, whether it was too small or otherwise, although, with his own permission, it was read to him a second time.

He commenced to state in detail the friendship that had existed between His Majesty's grandfather and the King of England, and stated that the country of Dahomey had not changed, but remained the same to this day.

We endeavoured to expostulate and explain to His Majesty the advantages that he must ultimately reap from agriculture, growing of cotton, as well as cultivating the palm-oil tree.

In reply the King stated that they were a warlike people, the Dahomians, and of course unaccustomed to agricultural pursuits; that he would not be able to keep up his revenues, were he at once to stop the Slave Trade. Being desirous that it should be stopped in the minor ports, prior to his entering into a treaty, requests that Her Majesty's Government will endeavour to blockade between Quittah and Lagos; and then he would endeavour to enter into an agreement for the suppression of the Slave Trade in His Majesty's own country. He asked if we had seen any farms between the swamp and Abomey? He could not disgrace himself and subject himself to be laughed at by sending the women from his Palace-yard to plant and cultivate cotton.

He also stated that he had taken and destroyed all the countries that formerly cultivated cotton.

We endeavoured to impress on His Majesty that if he employed the prisoners that were captured, instead of selling them out of their country, he might grow as much cotton as he pleased, and furthermore, England would buy it all from him and his people; however, he did not appear desirous to listen to any further discussions on agriculture.

His Majesty then requested us to address a letter to Her Majesty the Queen of England, his friend, that she would allow Whydah to become a free port; stating that he had five agents, mentioning at the same time their names, viz., Isidore, Ignacio, and Antonio—three sons of the late Da Souza—also Domingo Martins and Joaquim Antonio. His Majesty's simple request was to have papers and flags to allow them to pass without hindrance or molestation from Her Majesty's cruizers. Our reply was, that it was impossible. He appeared much perplexed, and harped upon the same theme for some time; at last His Majesty said, "Surely my friend the Queen of England will allow papers and colours for one vessel for myself to go free from the men-of-war." His pride must have fallen, when the great King of Dahomey condescended to ask for one vessel on similar terms as the five. When he found it impossible to induce us to change our theme, and write thus to the Queen of England, he felt much chagrined, and his countenance changed and became a shade lighter.

We then told him as he had declined the Queen of England's liberal offer, there was only the last resource, to go on the old plan and take his chance; that it was not within range of possibility that any favours could be shown His Majesty's vessels beyond the minor ports.

I then found that our mission was drawing to a close, and being determined to draw his attention to Abbeokuta, I asked his permission to allow me to read the Earl of Chichester's letter from the Queen to Sagbua, chief of the above-mentioned town. Finding the Queen's expressions of kindness to the chief so strong, with thanks for his kindness and protection to the missionaries etc., His Majesty appeared to be greatly excited and jealous, and said that he was going to war with that place; they were bad people; that the white men and ladies must be removed. I then told him that I was going to visit it as soon as the dry season set in, that would be about December. He then said, "You must take the Englishmen away from that place."

Mayogau, His Majesty's Prime Minister, made a very harsh remark, and said, "What right have the white men to go to and teach those fellows book palaver?"

His Majesty then said that when Freeman, from Cape Coast, visited Abomey, when he left he promised to send a white teacher, but he had not done so, neither had he heard any more on that matter.

He was then asked if a white missionary were sent to Abomey, would His Majesty afford him his protection and give him a grant of land to build a house; he replied in the affirmative, but he must reside at Whydah. It appears that he is averse to their residing at Abomey; but I really believe he was prompted by his Minister in a whisper to make that reply relative to the missionary residing at Whydah instead of Abomey.

I had another important request to lay before His Majesty with his permission, which was granted. I then stated that Mrs McCarthy, wife of John McCarthy, liberated Africans from Sierra Leone, late Ahguay, and residents of Whydah, complained to me that her husband, John McCarthy, was confined as a prisoner in His Majesty's court-yard; that he had been seized between Attahpam and Popo, on his route from the former to the latter. Not any person knew anything about the matter. I told the Cabooceer of Whydah, that he must know her; but he denied it. The King ordered the Mayogau to inquire into the affair. After which the Queen's despatch was read, and he made his mark; we witnessed it. He had not any more to say; only that he would communicate with me at Fernando Po, either by letter or a messenger, by any vessel that may be going that route from Whydah. It rained; we continued a short time, but no appearance of dry weather, we asked permission to depart. He said we must taste with him before we left; we went through the ceremony. He conducted us outside of the porch; shook hands. With his respects and best wishes for our safe arrivals at our different destinations, we left the Palace of Abomey for our own domicile. It rained the remainder of the day.

Next morning it was fine and dry. The King sent our presents for the road, of cowries, cloth, rum, etc., also a little girl each. After which we entered our house and held a short conference; present the Mayogau, Yavogau, and Narwhey, relative to Mr McCarthy: his wife was presented with her child. The Mayo said he would send her with a messenger to the home of the Cambodee, and they should both return here during the day. They asked when we intended to leave; we told them on the morrow, if we received a decisive answer about the man McCarthy. They said that was small palaver, and would soon be settled. They took their leave.

Next morning early the same party came again. We had to sit and hear the salutes fired; twenty-one guns for the Queen and thirteen for each of us, which took full two hours. After which the McCarthy question was again mooted; we stating that they did not make their appearance yesterday as they all, particularly the Mayogau, promised. The latter said that he sent her to the King yesterday, and that he sent her to the Cambodee's to see if her husband was there. I then told them, "I know from good authority that she is also a prisoner, but not with her husband; it is a farce; you are making fools of us." Commander Forbes expressed himself very warmly, and told them that he was going to England, and would report to the Queen that two British subjects were detained as prisoners in Abomey; at the same time he threw his memorandum-book on the table. They looked at him seriously, and said, "We hope you are not vexed; if so, we must tell our master the King." Rose and shook hands, and left us to take our breakfast before we started. A few packages being left detained us. Commander Forbes kindly offered to remain and start them off before him; and recommended me to leave for Cana. I left at 10 o'clock, and arrived at noon; half an hour afterwards Forbes joined. He remained to get a hammock and carriers for a sick man. I went on, and arrived at Tooboodoo at 2.20 PM. Commander Forbes did not arrive until 5 o'clock. During his detention a messenger arrived in post-haste, bringing with him McCarthy and his wife.

I presume they must have communicated the warm debate on the matter this morning; it shows a dread of the King's meeting the displeasure of Her Majesty's Government.

We started at 5 o'clock next morning; crossed the swamp, of which we had thirteen hours before we arrived at our halting-place. Ultimately arrived at Whydah on the 9th; found Her Majesty's sloop "Bonetta". "Gladiator" and "Jackal" arrived on the 11th. We succeeded in embarking through the surf on the 12th.

The King of Dahomey has been greatly exaggerated as to his wealth and power. I am perfectly satisfied that he is under the control and opinion of several of his principal officers; and it is too obvious that he has not the slightest desire to abandon the abominable Traffic.

The only effectual means to bring him to a full sense of his error, if international law will admit of it, is to take his own advice, and blockade Whydah.

Lagos is another point. If the legitimate chief could be seen and communicated with, so as to make a treaty with him for the suppression of the foreign Slave Trade, and place him at Lagos, his former seat of Government, it would release the people of Abbeokuta from the jeopardy that they are continually in, from the fear of the King of Dahomey.

Her Majesty's steamer "Gladiator" has captured two empty slavers. Her Majesty's steamer "Hecla" two with slaves, lately from Lagos. I believe they have been trying it hard there latterly.

Her Majesty's brig "Wolverene" took a felucca, two or three days ago.

I can only state that the King of Dahomey's power and wealth have been much exaggerated. As reported, he has 18,000 Amazons as a bodyguard; we have only seen and counted 3,000 and about the same number of men, at a grand review. He stated himself, the same day, that we did not see all his warriors; he had a great body guarding his frontiers. I estimate his army at 20,000 or 25,000.

His Majesty's account of his total expenditure of cowries for the year is only 42,000; his first account 32,000; about two-thirds more than we could account for.

I was anxious to get a just estimate of the number of tons of palm-oil shipped from Whydah etc., but I could not get any but exaggerated accounts, so I have declined making any statement at present, until my next visit at the latter end of the year.

AUGUST 1850

Commodore Fanshawe to the Secretary of the Admiralty
"Centaur", Cabenda, August 8, 1850

Sir,

With reference to my despatch of the 19th July, acquainting the Lords Commissioners of the Admiralty with the return of Mr Consul Beecroft and Lieutenant Forbes, of the "Bonetta", from their mission to Abomey, and transmitting Lieutenant Forbes's report, I have to request you will do me the honour to acquaint their Lordships that on conferring with Mr Beecroft on the subject of the King of Dahomey's declared intention of making the Abbeokuta Country the seat of his next war, I thought it desirable (in which opinion Mr Beecroft concurred) to address the letter to His Majesty, the copy of which I herewith enclose, and I hope my doing so will be approved of.

This letter was given to Mr Beecroft to transmit to the agent of Messrs Hutton's house at Whydah, in order to secure the King's having a proper knowledge of its purport, as well as the mercantile community of that place.

I beg you will also inform their Lordships that I have instructed the senior officer of the Bights Division, in the event of the missionaries at Badagry applying to him for powder and ball for their protection, to furnish it as far as he may be able.

ARTHUR FANSHAWE

Enclosure
Commodore Fanshawe to the King of Dahomey

To the most renowned King of Dahomey, the Commander-in-chief of the Squadron of Her Majesty the Queen of England on the coast of Africa, wishes health, peace, and the blessing of God.

"Centaur", Prince's Island, July 23, 1850

Sire,

I have learned with extreme regret, from Lieutenant Forbes, the officer of Her Majesty the Queen of England, my Sovereign, whom I sent to your capital of Abomey, that you have refused the proposals made to you by the directions of the Queen, to abandon the Traffic of Slaves in your dominions, and that you proposed making war on Abbeokuta, in the Yoruba Country, for the object of obtaining more slaves for sale.

It becomes my duty, therefore, to apprise you that the people of Yoruba are the friends of Her Majesty the Queen of England, and that Her Majesty's Government will see with much displeasure any act of violence or oppression committed against them; and also, that there are dwelling at Abbeokuta and in the Yoruba Country, many British-born subjects and liberated Africans, whom they are bound to protect from injury, and that if they receive any from your hands, it will be considered an act of hostility against the Queen and the English people, and will cause the coast of your Majesty's dominions to be immediately invested and blockaded by Her Majesty's ships under my command, and all trade stopped.

I hope your Majesty will come to some wiser conclusion, and that God may so dispose you.

ARTHUR FANSHAWE
Commander-in-chief of Her Britannic Majesty's Squadron
on the West Coast of Africa

OCTOBER 1850

Mr Hutton to Viscount Palmerston (received October 10)
Watling Street, October 8, 1850

My Lord,

I have received a letter from Cape Coast, dated on the 7th August last, written by a nephew of mine who has been a resident on the coast of Africa during the last twenty years, the contents of which, so far as they relate to the reasons and motives of the King of Dahomey for evading or refusing to enter into a Treaty for the suppression of the Slave Trade, I feel desirous that your Lordship should be acquainted with; and if it has happened that Commander Forbes and Mr Beecroft, who visited that chief in July last, were unsuccessful in obtaining his assent to a formal treaty, and were not informed by him of the causes of objection, the information I relay will be considered of sufficient importance to excuse my sending your Lordship the letter itself instead of an extract from it.

W. M. HUTTON

At a convenient opportunity your Lordship will doubtless do me the favour to let me have the letter back again.

Enclosure

Mr Thomas Hutton to Mr Hutton
Cape Coast, August 7, 1850

My dear Uncle,

The great interest you have at all times taken for the welfare of this country, and your efforts in regard to the suppression of the Slave Trade, induced me to let you know what fell under my observation in my recent visit to Whydah and that neighbourhood.

M. da Souza, the notorious slave-dealer, died, as you are aware, about fifteen months ago; this man was in his 81st year when he died. He went to Whydah in the year 1792, in his 24th year. Various have been the rumours that occasioned his going there; he, however, himself once told me he came out as Secretary under the Portuguese Government to their fort in Whydah, and remained three years in that service, and then returned to the Brazils where I imagined he was born. He wished it supposed that he was a Spaniard by birth, and was always treated so in courtesy and styled Don. The Portuguese did not long continue to support their Government in Whydah, and the Slave Trade there soon fell into the hands of the most enterprising, the most so of whom was M. da Souza. He had for many years an extraordinary run of good luck, and it was imagined had amassed a large fortune. His fame as a slave-dealer gained him unlimited credit in the Havana and Brazil, and ship after ship arrived from those places at Popo, Whydah and Lagos, consigned to him generally with full cargoes of merchandise and specie; the goods were recklessly landed in bamboo store-houses on the beach. It was presumed no native dare rob him; in this, however, he was mistaken, as there is now no doubt about the matter.

The accumulated cargoes brought upon him an immense amount of debt; of this he appeared utterly regardless so long as it had the desired effect upon the natives to cause them to consider him possessed of inexhaustible wealth, and for the King of Dahomey to imagine the same, on whom he lavished vast sums of wealth, but who in return could never at any time supply more than a fraction of the amount in slaves for the large amount of property that was sent to him; and frequently from 30 to 40 ships in the year 1826 were lying in the Roadsteads of Whydah, all consigned to Da Souza, who had landed all their cargoes, but in return could seldom supply more than four or five cargoes of slaves. Many of the ships after staying out twenty months to two years, from their light construction went to pieces on the beach; others lost all their crews and were abandoned; some became prizes, and the general result was, as no account whatever was kept of cargoes landed, every species of extravagance and expenditure took place, to the ruin of the owners. Some of them sent out supercargoes to see what the former were about. Frequently the fate of the second supercargo and ship and cargo went the way of the first. So lucrative, however, was the profit on slaves, or the want of them so much required, that some years elapsed before these reckless consignees to Da Souza began to grow cautious, in fact, not before many were ruined. In the interim a more rigid law had passed respecting the capture of slave-trading vessels.

The King of Dahomey, who thus had had for years past countless wealth poured in upon him, became at last exacting when the rapid torrent ceased to flow so fast as formerly, and it took some years before he could in the least comprehend the causes that had diminished the supplies to his agent Da Souza, who had years before virtually become so; to have the monopoly of the Trade and who went annually to Dahomey with tribute to the King, and with vast supplies to his chiefs, to furnish them with means for the next slave-hunt. Year after year these supplies became gradually less, Da Souza having become gradually poorer, and troubled with a host of creditors in the Havana and Brazils. The principals, or consignees themselves, in many instances, came to Whydah to claim their debts. Da Souza keeping no accounts, generally denied all knowledge of the parties or the business on which they had come about; frequently he would absent himself or be in Dahomey months, when a party of creditors arrived from the Havana or Brazils. Yet such was the nature of the Trade, a lucky voyage or two enabled him to pacify the clamours of these distressed creditors. He treated them with country presents and an unbounded hospitality, and with tales of the endless resources of the King, who would at any time send him as many slaves as he pleased.

Various enactments took place, and the cruizers were more vigilant than ever, and matters grew worse and worse. Merchants in the Havana sent agents to have interviews with the King; heavy complaints were made against Da Souza, which, for policy sake, the King would not listen to, he himself not being the rightful successor, but upheld by Da Souza's influence and vast presents to the chiefs.

At last, after a few more years, it was arranged that agents from the Havana and Brazils might settle at Whydah, and Da Souza should give up shipping slaves, but to receive a commission of a doubloon for every slave that was shipped. On this he lived in the latter years of his life. He had also raised up duties or contributions on every native who held a slave, at per head, which enabled him latterly to keep up some appearance before the King and his chiefs; but this grew less and less, until he actually became tortured with the thought of want. When he died his stores were empty. The King of Dahomey sent to have his property taken up to him, and his chiefs entered into the house, and all that could be found was simply a little furniture and some plate; but neither money, goods, nor anything of value. This lesson has been most salutary to the King and his chiefs, to see that the man whom they considered was possessed of endless wealth, had died without the value of a keg of gunpowder in his stores to be fired over his remains, which is with them considered extreme poverty; thus confounding them, and shaking their confidence in the stability of the Slave Trade. Such was the end of one of the greatest slave-dealers of modern times.

Da Souza may be considered to have been the mainspring of the Slave Trade on that part of the coast; his long life, influence, and slave-trading notoriety, has given way, and his like is not likely to be replaced. The recklessness of the Havana and Brazilian consignees has ceased to flow to Whydah, and the stream of wealth in consequence has ceased to flow to Dahomey. This has curtailed the King's means to make extraordinary slave-hunts; and so great have been the recent changes, by the introduction of palm-oil and other legitimate commerce, combined with the vigilance of the cruizers, that the Slave Trade is being cut up root and branch; and if it was not for the feeling of being lowered in the eyes of the surrounding nations, it is supposed the King would most willingly give it up, as he has created so many hostile powers against himself; and the free trade in palm-oil that has extended all along that coast has enabled every petty state or tribe to furnish themselves with arms and ammunition against the common enemy, who was formerly the only power who could get them.

The King well knows how everything is working against him, and he feels the loss of his ancient friend and counsellor, Da Souza. One thing alone is wanting to compel him to stop the Trade, that is, to get possession of Lagos, and either by treaty or force utterly extinguish the Slave Trade there. The King of Dahomey says, if that is done, he will then be willing to listen to a treaty: he adds, "Why do you send up to me, who live so far from the sea-side, to stop the Slave Trade, and the King of Lagos, who lives on the sea-side, is not questioned or stopped, nor any notice taken of what he does? First stop him on the sea-side, and then, as the Slave Trade only exists between Popo and Lagos, being once stopped, I shall have no excuse but to submit to a treaty, if your cruizers compel me; but until the Slave Trade at Lagos is stopped either by treaty or by force, my chiefs will not listen to any proposition I may make towards its suppression."

The King of Dahomey sent to me several times when I was at Whydah, to go up to him, as he had something to say to me. With much difficulty I got myself excused; I had important matters to attend to at Badagry, and the rainy season being near at hand, I had no time to lose. I made the King perfectly aware of this, that no misunderstanding or ill-feeling should arise in his mind; and he then sent me a private and friendly message, and one of his confidential friends told me what I have stated above, that unless the Slave Trade is first put a stop to at Lagos, it will be useless for the British Government to send to him treaties for his agreement, as he considers it would be derogatory to his dignity, and would lower him in the eyes of his subjects and the nations around, who would not be able to understand the reason that an interior King should be the first that is made to stop the Slave Trade, while the sea-side King of Lagos, so near to come at, is not even spoken to on the subject, and carries on the Trade as if he was sanctioned in it.

If the English get possession of Lagos, there is an immediate blow to the Abbeokutian and Benin Slave Trade; and the good that would then ensue to those countries is incalculable, as they abound in cotton, indigo, palm-oil, and many other resources for industry and wealth. There would be little or no difficulty in the achievement in taking Lagos, and the best time of the year for it would be from November to February, the season is then fine and whole-some, and continues so until May, when the rains set-in, with the exception of the tornadoes in March. The latter rains falling in September, would render the Cradoo Lagoon to be deeper, as well as the entrance or Bar of Lagos, which, during those months, is quite smooth. The town Onim, or the capital of Lagos, where the King resides, is situated on the Island of Lagos, just at the entrance of the Cradoo.

THOMAS HUTTON

Viscount Palmerston to Consul Beecroft
Foreign Office, October 11, 1850

Sir,

I have received your despatch of the 22nd of July, reporting your proceedings on your mission to Abomey.

Her Majesty's Government much regret the failure of your endeavours to induce the King of Dahomey to enter into a treaty for the suppression of the Slave Trade; which failure, however, appears to be by no means attributable to any want of diligence, or zeal, or efforts either on your part of that of Lieutenant Forbes.

Her Majesty's Government are also much concerned at learning that the King of Dahomey has expressed an inten-tion of going to war with the Chiefs of Abbeokuta; and I have accordingly addressed a letter to the King upon these matters, which I have to instruct you to cause to be transmitted to him at an early moment and by a safe conveyance.

I enclose for your information a copy of this letter.

I at the same time enclose, for your information, a copy of a letter which, by my direction, has been addressed to the Admiralty, containing recommendations as to the steps to be taken for putting a stop to Slave Trade at Lagos; and at the other slave-trading ports which lie between that place and Quittah.

PALMERSTON

Enclosure 1

Viscount Palmerston to the King of Dahomey
Foreign Office, October 11, 1850

Sir,

I am commanded by Her Majesty to acknowledge the receipt of the letter which you addressed to her on the 4th of July last; and I have in the first place to beg you to accept the best thanks of the British Government for the very kind and hospitable manner in which you received Mr Beecroft and Commander Forbes during their late visit to your Majesty's capital of Abomey; and I beg to assure you, Sir, that this friendly conduct on your part has still more increased the earnest desire of the British Government to cultivate the most intimate relations between the Kingdoms of Great Britain and of Dahomey.

But as nothing more contributes to the maintenance of friendship than a frank explanation of mutual feelings and opinions, I deem it of importance to advert to the statement which you made to Mr Beecroft that you intended to make war upon the Chiefs of Abbeokuta; and I feel it right to inform you that the Queen of England takes a great interest in favour of that city and its people, and that if you value the friendship of England, you will abstain from any attack upon and from any hostility against that town and people.

The British Government would be very sorry that you should make such an attack: first, because Her Majesty's Government would deeply regret that any evil should happen to the people of Abbeokuta; and secondly, because Her Majesty's Government would feel much concern if anything should be done by your Majesty which would lead to an interruption of the friendly relations between yourself and the Government of England.

With respect to what you have written about the Slave Trade, the British Government is much disappointed at your answer, for they had hoped and expected that you would have complied with their very reasonable request, accompanied as it was by a handsome offer of full compensation for any temporary loss which you might sustain by putting an end to the Slave Trade. But as you have declined to consent to what the British Government has asked you to do, the British Government will be obliged to employ its own means to accomplish its purpose; and as England is sure to succeed in any object which it is determined to attain, the result will be, that the Slave Trade from Dahomey will be put an end to by the British cruisers, and thus you will sustain the temporary loss of revenue without receiving the offered compensation. But it is at least a satisfaction to Her Majesty's Government to think that your loss of revenue will only be felt by you for a short time, and that the profits which will arise to you from legal commerce will soon very amply repay you for any deficiency of revenue created by the cessation of Slave Trade.

PALMERSTON

Enclosure 2

Mr Addington to the Secretary of the Admiralty
Foreign Office, October 11, 1850

Sir,

I am directed by Viscount Palmerston to transmit to you the accompanying copy of a despatch from Mr Beecroft [July 22, 1850], Her Majesty's Consul in the Bights of Benin and Biafra, reporting the failure of his endeavours to induce the King of Dahomey to enter into a treaty for the suppression of the Slave Trade, and stating that the King of Dahomey had expressed an intention of making war on the Chiefs of Abbeokuta. I am to transmit to you also a copy of a letter [July 4, 1850] addressed by the King of Dahomey to Her Majesty, stating his views with respect to the Slave Trade.

I am to request that you will lay these papers before the Lords Commissioners of the Admiralty, and that you will state to their Lordships that it appears to Lord Palmerston that it seems clear that the King of Dahomey will not be induced to enter into any agreement to abandon Slave Trade until the Chief of Lagos shall have previously been brought to enter into such an enagement, and until Slave Trade shall have been effectually stopped at Whydah.

It seems, therefore, to Lord Palmerston, that measures should forthwith be resorted to for the purpose of putting an end to Slave Trade at Lagos, and that with this view the present Chief of Lagos should be invited to enter into an engagement similar to that which was agreed to by the chiefs at Gallinas; and if he should refuse to do so, that measures similar to those which were enforced against Gallinas, should be brought to bear upon Lagos, or that steps should be taken to replace in authority at Lagos the former chief, who is understood to be now at Badagry, and who would, it is believed, willingly subscribe to the proposed engagement.

In the meantime it would be desirable that the strictest watch which circumstances might admit of should be established, to prevent slaves from being exported from Whydah.

It is obvious that the King of Dahomey, who is the greatest originator of Slave Trade in that part of Africa in which his territory lies, will yield, in regard to that Trade, only when compelled by necessity to do so, and when he shall be quite sure that the profits which he would give up by relinquishing that pursuit, would not pass into the hands of any less conceding neighbour.

I enclose for their Lordships' information, a copy of a letter which Viscount Palmerston has addressed to the King of Dahomey on this matter.

H. U. ADDINGTON

Commodore Fanshawe to the Secretary of the Admiralty
"Centaur", at sea, Lat. 4° 58′ N., Long. 4° 2′ E.
October 28, 1850

Sir,

My letter to you of the 15th instant will have informed the Lords Commissioners of the Admiralty, that having communicated with Mr Beecroft, Her Majesty's Consul at Fernando Po, I was about to proceed to Badagry, for the purpose of ascertaining from the missionaries at that place, what would be the position and wants both of themselves and their establishment at Abbeokuta, in case the King of Dahomey should execute his threat of making the Yoruba Country the scene of his next war and slave-hunt.

I have now the honour to request you will inform their Lordships that I anchored off Badagry on the 21st, and sent Lieutenant Boys, of this ship, on shore, with a letter to Mr Gollmer, in charge of the church mission; and also to examine what assistance it might be practicable for the cruizers to render, if required, and that I have the satisfaction of learning by Mr Gollmer's reply to me, a copy of which I beg to enclose for their Lordships' information, as well as from Lieutenant Boys' report, that the present position of their Christian establishments was one of comparative security, which was likely to be confirmed by my arrival in the roads and communication with them, and Lieutenant Boys visiting the chiefs; and that I have given to Captain Adams, of the "Gladiator", the senior officer of the division, instructions to meet the wishes of the missionaries as far as practicable, until the period for the Dahomian war is past.

I ascertained from Captain Adams, that my letter to the King of Dahomey, on the subject of his war on Abbeokuta, a copy of which I have already forwarded for their Lordships' information, was landed at Whydah last month for transmission through the means of Mr Hastie, the agent of Messrs Hutton; but as that gentleman has been since unfortunately drowned, I have not been able to learn whether it reached His Majesty. No canoes are now permitted to come off to our men-of-war at Whydah.

I have availed myself of this visit to the Bights to communicate with all the cruizers of the division, and I am happy to inform their Lordships that I have found them all healthy, for I hope the "Gladiator" need not longer be considered an exception. I have also anchored off Quittah and Whydah, and am now returning to Prince's Island and the South Coast, to meet the "Niger" and the September mail.

ARTHUR FANSHAWE

Enclosure

Messrs Gollmer and Van Cooten to Commodore Fanshawe
Church Mission House, Badagry, October 22, 1850

Sir,

We beg to acknowledge the receipt of your kind letter of yesterday's date, and to express that we all, myself and brother missionaries, British merchants and liberated

Africans, here, are greatly indebted to you for the very lively interest you take in our behalf, and the essential service you have rendered to us by the kind measures you have adopted, in sending ships of war to inquire as to our safety, and your own timely appearance.

The position of our own friends at Abbeokuta, the Rev. H. Townsend and Mrs Townsend, the Rev. J. Smith and Mrs Smith, the Rev. D. Hinderer, with our native missionary, the Rev. S. Crowther, and the large band of native Christians, is comparatively a safe one, as they can rely on the protection of almost all the powerful chiefs and people at that place. Mr Townsend, however, to whom I will forward your esteemed letter, will no doubt avail himself of your kind request to inform you as to their real position.

As regards ourselves at Badagry, where the majority of the chiefs and people are greatly influenced and stimulated by the slave-traders, we can scarcely tell what is our true position, and what to-morrow will bring forth: some are friendly, and many would expel us, if we were not protected by the ships of war; but we do believe (or hope) that the frequently appearing of ships of war in our roads, and an occasional visit from Her Majesty's officers, will deter them from doing us any harm.

It is astonishing the effect created in our town by the appearing of a ship of war, by the visit of an officer, or even by the firing of a few guns.

In accordance with your kind offer to render us any assistance we may deem desirable as regards our safety, we would request the favour, if convenient, to instruct ships of war frequently to call in here, so that in case of danger we may receive their protection; that we may be visited by Her Majesty's officers; and that a few guns may be fired, as if exercising; and may we request that you will now favour us by discharging a few guns, which we trust will have the anticipated effect upon those who are still inimical to us.

This is the only assistance we, for the present, deem necessary, and therefore beg to decline your offer to supply us with arms and ammunition.

As regards the Dahomian invasion, we know so much, that Dahomey has an old grudge against the town especially, and would unquestionably destroy it if British residents were removed. We therefore do not know whether we shall be molested from that quarter or not.

The marauding expeditions of Dahomey generally take place during the months of December and January, and we would request the favour that our position may be remembered by you during that time.

In conclusion we beg to return our sincere thanks for your great kindness to us and to our work, in helping us to maintain our position, and thus furthering the holy cause in which we are engaged; it it truly encouraging to us to be thus supported. May the blessing of God rest upon you and your endeavours to ameliorate our poor benighted sable brethren.

C. A. GOLLMER
E. C. VAN COOTEN

P.S. The Wesleyan ministry has gone to Cape Coast for a short time.

DECEMBER 1850

*The Rev. Henry Townsend to Captain H. D. Trotter
(communicated to Viscount Palmerston by Captain Trotter,
April 7, 1851)*

(Extract)   *Abbeokuta, December* 10, 1850

We have been graciously preserved here hitherto. The reports of the intentions of the King of Dahomey have reached us, but it excites very little alarm among the people. They have destroyed a town reputed to have been under Dahomian influence, and for that reason, in truth I believe, they have all but made a clear sweep of the towns and villages between this and Porto Novo; and I fear they will not stop until some reverse teaches them to be moderate.

The Slave Trade I understand to be pretty much the same as I last stated. It has been a peculiarly unfortunate year for that nefarious Traffic, through the watchfulness of Her Majesty's cruizers. I hope we are on the eve of better times, and that yet we shall completely triumph over the Slave Trade.

Mr Gollmer has had frequent communication with the cruizers, and they have manifested great concern for our safety since hearing of the King of Dahomey's intentions. The Commodore called off Badagry and wrote to us twice about it; we wrote a long letter in return, bringing him acquainted with the entire state of things here.

The Government here is exceedingly weak; it is just as if all the German principalities and little kingdoms were brought together into one town, each bringing their separate institutions and Governments, and acting but seldom in union; therefore we have the strange sight of an active persecution in one part of the town, while in another there is not even an attempt at such. It has broken out again in Mr Crowther's district, but it is to be hoped that it will not last long.

It will not appear strange to you that the chief of the persecutors is also chief of the slave-traders; and there is another circumstance that has some connection, viz., that the last market-day was peculiarly unfortunate, and many slaves brought back unsold. The slave-traders then attempted to take away the merchandise that our converts had purchased in lawful trade, being enraged with the fact that they with slaves could not purchase, while our people without could. They were accused and abused for favouring the English, the spoilers of the Slave Trade. It is said that three months' purchase of slaves are in Lagos unable to be shipped, and some dying for want. My informants told me that the same trader who purchased slaves at 50 dollars the market before, offered only 40 dollars now; but at what price a purchase was effected they could not tell. I feel inclined to think that now is the time to endeavour to introduce a better trade there.

I have had a long conversation this morning with some of the people exposed to the persecution lately broke out again, with a view of getting from them their view of the cause of it; and they told me distinctly and upon sufficient grounds, that while the idol-worship is the assigned, the real reason is the Slave Trade; and that it all comes from Lagos. Their ultimate object is to get rid of the white man; but as it cannot be accomplished by direct means, they seek to do it by drawing away those who become Christians—supposing, I think, that we receive pay for every convert; and that when the hope of gain is gone, we shall go away.

> *Viscount Palmerston to Mr Fraser*
> *Foreign Office, December* 10, 1850

My Lord,

I have to acquaint you that Her Majesty's Government have been pleased to select you to be British Vice-Consul within the territories of the King of Dahomey, on the western coast of Africa, in the place of the late Mr John Duncan.

I herewith enclose a formal letter of authority under my hand and seal to enable you to act as such.

The objects which Her Majesty's Government have in view in this appointment are fully explained in the annexed instructions, which were given to the late Vice-Consul Duncan, and which were returned to this office after Mr Duncan's death.

You will consider those instructions as addressed to yourself, and you will take them as the rule of your conduct during the time you shall act as British Vice-Consul in Dahomey.

PALMERSTON

Viscount Palmerston to Consul Beecroft
Foreign Office, December 11, 1850

Sir,

I have to state to you that Her Majesty's Government have appointed Mr Louis Fraser to be British Vice-Consul at Whydah, within the territories of the King of Dahomey, on the western coast of Africa.

I transmit to you a copy of the instructions which I have given to Vice-Consul Fraser; and I have to direct you to keep up an unreserved communication with him, and to give him such advice and instructions for his guidance as may appear to you to be right and proper for the good of Her Majesty's service.

I have sent a copy of this letter to Vice-Consul Fraser.

PALMERSTON

JANUARY–FEBRUARY 1851

The Rev. C. A. Gollmer to Captain H. D. Trotter (communicated to Viscount Palmerston by Captain Trotter, April 7)

(Extract)   *Badagry, January* 13, 1851

The thermometer of religious inquiry and anxiety is still low. Knowledge increases, and conviction of right and wrong may be observed as its offspring, here and there; but of new creatures, the fruit of the Holy Spirit, which we long to see, we cannot speak. The thermometer of iniquitous agitation, on the contrary, stands still high, yea, of late, it rose here to "fever heat", which, had God not watched over us, might have consumed us. Twice our town was nigh being burnt down by the Lagos people here, who were about doing so in revenge upon the Popos, who, since the last few months, have, contrary to an existing law, gone to

Lagos and are determined to open the road, and trade with Lagos, which Akitoye★ will not allow, as it renders his residence here unsafe: however, the Popos, the last few weeks, went down in so numerous a party, that it was difficult to oppose the movement. We still fear one of these days we shall suddenly be alarmed with war and destruction. The town we of course keep quite neutral. Yet often we are consulted, when we advise peace.

Captain Beecroft, Her Britannic Majesty's Consul, has at last arrived, on the 2nd of January, and was received with honours here. On the 7th he went to Abbeokuta with Mr Van Cooten, and I have just heard of their safe arrival, and how white and black chiefs went to meet him some eight miles on the way, and showed him much honour. We hope much good will ensue from this visit. If only our merchants would be more one with us, and not for filthy lucre's sake cherish and nourish what is the curse of this country; these gents, of course, do not want to see a Consul, one who will report their proceedings. Mr Hutton was down, and his vessel sold a cargo, I believe powder, at Lagos, and Mr Hutton himself went to Lagos to do business. The Consul is in favour of Akitoye, the expelled rightful King of Lagos, who petitions him for the Government to take Lagos, plant the British flag there and establish him under it, and he will make a Treaty to abolish all Slave Trade and carry on only lawful traffic. I trust the Government will take it up, for Lagos is certainly the focus of the Slave Trade, and will be a great acquisition, especially for missionary operations.

The Slave Trade is not only greatly checked, but nearly done for; the slave-traders are nearly mad on account of the Brazilian laws respecting the Trade, and the vigilance and close blockade of our cruizers; it may be that we shall have

★The legitimate but expelled Chief of Lagos, who lives at Badagry, or very near it.

to suffer. The converts at Abbeokuta in one district are persecuted in consequence of the Slave Trade being spoilt at Lagos. Of 137 slaves, Mr Townsend tells me only 7 were purchased the other day.

> *Lord Stanley of Alderley to the Secretary of the Admiralty*
> *Foreign Office, February* 10, 1851

Sir,

I laid before Viscount Palmerston Commodore Fanshawe's despatch of the 28th of October; and with reference to the doubt therein expressed by the Commodore, whether the letter which he addressed to the King of Dahomey on the 23rd of July, 1850, on the subject of the alleged intention of the King to make war upon Abbeokuta, had been forwarded to His Majesty, I am to request you to state to the Lords Commissioners of the Admiralty, that Lord Palmerston is of opinion that it would be important to ascertain whether the letter in question was sent on to the King or not; and if it was not sent, it would be right that a copy or duplicate thereof should be forwarded to him.

STANLEY OF ALDERLEY

> *Viscount Palmerston to Consul Beecroft*
> *Foreign Office, February* 20, 1851

Sir,

On the 22nd of April last I suggested to the Lords Commissioners of the Admiralty that the next step which it seemed desirable to take, with a view to clear the African coast north of the Equator from Slave Trade, would be to induce the Chief of Lagos to conclude a treaty for the abolition of that Traffic.

I have not yet heard whether any communication has been made to the Chief of Lagos, in pursuance of my recommendation above alluded to. But if, when this despatch reaches you, the Chief of Lagos should not have bound himself by treaty to abolish Slave Trade, you will put yourself in communication with that chief, with a view to induce him to conclude a treaty in the form which I herewith transmit to you, and you will concert with Commodore Fanshawe the best arrangements for the execution of this service.

The Commodore will be instructed to furnish you with the means of carrying on this negotiation without placing yourself hazardously in the power of that chief. I have also to authorize and instruct you to conclude treaties according to the standard form, with any native chiefs within the limits of your Consular district, whose co-operation for the suppression of Slave Trade you may consider it desirable to obtain.

PALMERSTON

Viscount Palmerston to Consul Beecroft
Foreign Office, February 21, 1851

Sir,

With reference to my despatch of the 20th instant, in which I authorized you to conclude a Treaty for the abolition of the Slave Trade with the Chief of Lagos, I have now further to instruct you to represent to that Chief that the British Government is resolved to put an end to the African Slave Trade, and has the means and power to do so. That it is employing those means with increasing success on both sides of the Atlantic. That the British Government has been successfully urging the Governments of Spain and of the Brazils to prevent the importation of slaves into Cuba and into Brazil, and that thus the demand for slaves will be greatly diminished, if not entirely put an end to; while, on the other hand, the British Government has made treaties with the greater part of the native chiefs on the west coast of Africa, by which those chiefs have engaged to put an end to the exportation of slaves from within the limits of their territorial authority, and to encourage lawful commerce instead of Slave Trade.

You will represent that lawful commerce is more advantageous to the nations of Africa than Slave Trade, and that, therefore, the British Government in putting down Slave Trade, and in encouraging lawful commerce, is conferring a benefit upon the people and chiefs of Africa. That Great Britain is a strong Power both by sea and by land; that her friendship is worth having; and that her displeasure it is well to avoid. That the friendship of Great Britain is to be obtained by the Chiefs of Africa only on the condition that they abandon Slave Trade and expel the slave-traders, and that those chiefs who may refuse to do these things will surely incur the displeasure of the British Government.

If the Chief should show a disposition to refuse compliance, you should beg him to remember that Lagos is near to the sea, and that on the sea are the ships and the cannon of England; and also to bear in mind that he does not hold his authority without a competitor, and that the chiefs of the African tribes do not always retain their authority to the end of their lives.

PALMERSTON

Consul Beecroft to Viscount Palmerston (received June 10)
(Extract)   *Clarence, Fernando Po, February* 21, 1851
I have the honour to communicate to your Lordship a brief detail of my visit to Badagry and Abbeokuta.

During my stay at Badagry I had a private interview with Akitoye, the ex-King of Lagos. He is a quite prudent man, to all appearances; and from what was communicated to me by Mr Gollmer and himself, it is too obvious that there is a league formed with Kosoko, his nephew, the present Ruler of Lagos, and the Popos of Badagry, against Akitoye, so far advanced, that his life is in danger, indeed he has offered a premium for his head. Akitoye has a great number of followers, and they are kept continually under arms.

I have advised him to keep peace, unless attacked, until I returned from Abbeokuta, and that he must write me a full statement of his grievances; that I intended to-morrow to convene a meeting of the chiefs of Badagry, ten in number, with himself. I sent a messenger with my ring, accordingly, requesting the different chiefs to attend a conference held by me, Rev. Gollmer, and Dr Van Cooten, at 10 o'clock to-morrow.

It was noon before they were all assembled. I read to them my commission, after which other small matters were discussed. I then addressed them relative to Kosoko of Lagos tampering with some parties relative to a person of note under their protection, and I considered it their imperative duty to protect him to the last. They denied having any communication with Kosoko on that matter. I told them that I was going in a day or two to start for Abbeokuta; that I strongly impressed upon them, whatever they did, to preserve peace, which they faithfully promised to do; that on my return from Abbeokuta we should meet again; so the conference broke up. One of the parties present, called Mayen, ex-King of Porto Novo, is a staunch friend of Akitoye's; they are afraid of the two parties and the Popos, the instruments of Kosoko. My Lord, you must be aware that the road to Lagos from Badagry has been shut since Akitoye was expelled; now the Popos have opened it, contrary to his wish, and they are combining with his enemies to destroy him; now the road is open he is not safe. I strongly advised Akitoye to have patience and a still tongue, until my return from Abbeokuta, which he faithfully promised to do.

I left Badagry on the 7th ultimo, accompanied by Dr Van Cooten, and arrived at Awiyadee on the 9th, ten miles from Abbeokuta, where he remained all night.

Next morning at 10 o'clock we were joined by the Revs H. Townsend, Smith, Crowther, Church missionaries, and Mr Bickersteth, Wesleyan Society. They were rejoiced to meet me. After a light refreshment we started at 10.30, and arrived at the river. At 11.30 waited some time for the arrival of Mr Townsend. We started and crossed the stream; it will be about 500 yards wide when at its height in the centre, and in a great part in crossing at this season of the year there were two feet depth. We entered the walls of the town at 10 o'clock. I was certainly astonished when such a mass of houses presented themselves; I was informed that I only saw a small part of the town; I replied it contains more near 120,000 souls than fifty. I was shown as the Lion, and paraded through the longest part of the town, and arrived at Mr Townsend's compound at 3.30. I was warmly and cordially received by Mr and Mrs Townsend.

January 11. At daylight I accompanied Mr Townsend to the summit of a mass of granite and feldspar; found the interstices in a decomposed state, and vegetation going on. There is a good view, but the morning was hazy. I sent messengers to Sagbua; they returned, and stated that he had heard that I had made peace at Badagry, but still he was afraid that Akitoye would suffer, and it is certain the King of Dahomey was coming. He said he would call on me privately to-night to see me; it is not his desire that all we know should be made public or exposed to some of the public members of the Council. During the day Rev. I. Smith called; it is about two or two and a half miles to his compound.

Sagbua, the head chief, sent a messenger to Mr Townsend, stating that he was at liberty, that he would be glad to see him and the stranger. Accordingly we went, accompanied by all our friends. On our arrival I saluted the chief as a messenger of peace from my mistress the Queen of England; he returned the salute very graciously, and enquired kindly after Her Majesty and all the Royal Family; if they were well when I left England; he then said he was more than glad to see me at Abbeokuta, and trusted that God would long spare me for the sake of Africa. I then told him, as it was late, I merely called to pay my respects. I then spoke a few words, and told him that I was very anxious that he should announce to all his war-chiefs and traders, that I wished to have a conference as early in next week as possible. I got up to take my leave; he said he must rise to salute me: he was the father of the white men here before my arrival; that I was his father. I thanked him for the compliment and took our leave.

In the evening Sagbua and a few of his attendants waited on me. After the first salutation he intimated through the interpreter, that it was his desire that our party should be private, with the exception of two or three of his confidential attendants; we accordingly adjourned to my private room, accompanied by Mr Townsend. I then communicated my errand to Abbeokuta, as a messenger of peace, and to consult upon the best means to arrest this abominable Traffic—the foreign Slave Trade, and to introduce legitimate trade. He immediately commenced upon Lagos and Kosoko, the present chief and usurper, and said he was a bad man; that matters could never go on peaceably with him at the head as ruler; that he paid great sums of cowries to several slave-dealers in districts of Abbeokuta, to get them to set their face against and persecute the missionaries at Badagry and here, and told them if they were sent away, he would send slave-vessels to anchor off Badagry to take slaves; he sent presents also to the King of Dahomey, to induce him to raise war against Abbeokuta; which is the occasion of harassing them very much every dry season, his people being deterred from visiting their farms on that very account.

Guezo, the King of Dahomey, his continued threats render them anxious and desirous that he should come and try his skill with them in one of their open grass-fields, and decide the matter; Sagbua said his Egbas must and would fight hard for their all, for they had not any back-doors, for they were beset with enemies to the eastward, the Jebos bordering on Benin, instruments in the hands of Kosoko of Lagos. He said the Egbas were most anxious for legitimate trade, and too anxious that the above-mentioned place should be wrested from the usurper, and Akitoye, the right chief, in his proper position, and under the protection of the British flag, or otherwise, as Her Majesty's Government should deem fit; all would go on right. A canoe can communicate with Lagos in one night, and ascend to Abbeokuta in two days, on the River Ogu. I then communicated to him my visit to the King of Dahomey, and what passed relative to Abbeokuta. He was much pleased, but all his sentiments were relative to Lagos and placing Akitoye on the throne as before; all would go right; he was ready with his chiefs to enter into any Treaty the English Government pleased to dictate. His sentiments do not differ in the smallest relative to the abominable Traffic in Slaves; all his chiefs were anxious to leave it off—only a few of the creatures of that fellow Kosoko here, to our great annoyance. I then again reminded him that I was anxious to have an interview and a conference. He promised it should be arranged for the beginning of the week, this being Saturday. He desired me not to mention at the public conference any matters about Kosoko; I was at perfect liberty to state all other matters on the subject of the Slave Trade and my visit to Abomey. I told him on some subjects I should be obliged to speak aloud; he said I was right. He expressed himself much pleased with his interview, and desired to take leave. After family prayers retired to rest.

January 12. *Sunday.* Visited the church, morning and afternoon; it was full, there were about 200 hearers. Mr Townsend read the Church Service in the Yoruba tongue, the sermon was communicated through an interpreter. It was really interesting to hear the little dark creatures lisping their Maker's praises; it was delightful to see the solemnity of the little church, and so well attended; he will have to enlarge it soon. It is a very comfortable building, walls of switch and mud, with a high thatch roof, and well ventilated.

January 14. *Tuesday.* After breakfast some of the chiefs commenced their parade towards the grand square, near Chief Sagbua's mansion; it was close to Mr Townsend's compound. One of the elders named Lara called on me. 11 o'clock, drums and umbrellas were seen advancing in the distance towards the grand square where the conference was to be held; near the council-chamber there were several shady trees. It was 12 o'clock when our procession arrived at the place; chairs and benches had been placed near the shade of a large tree. I was placed in a large arm-chair, and in full uniform, but not pleasing; the thermometer 95°. To the right all the war-chiefs, about twenty; to the left, under the verandah of the council-house, Sagbua and the commercial community; a great host of spectators, including a great number of Sierra Leone emigrants. After saluting them, the Rev. H. Townsend introduced me in a short and appropriate speech, relative to my visit, and of its being previously communicated to the chiefs etc. Trusted they would listen to my counsel, and duly appreciate the Queen of England and her Government's kind intentions towards them. Reverend friend sat down. I then stood up and read my commission; it was interpreted by the Rev. S. Crowther, after which I thanked them in the name of Her Britannic

Majesty and her Government, for the kind protection afforded to God's messengers, and mentioned that they must be well aware that there cannot exist any other motive than a just and pure one, in being anxious to serve the sons and daughters of Africa; it is too obvious when they look upon all those people that have returned to their relatives and families, after a very long absence, and the fact of their being released from thraldom, and nourished and cherished by the English for a number of years; some have returned to their families and friends rich; it is only the English that have shown such a strong desire to renovate and reform Africa, and pull it out of the awful darkness that overshadows it. Her example has obliged other nations to step in to her aid.

I then communicated my visit to the King of Dahomey, and what transpired during my residence of six weeks there, and all that was said relative to Abbeokuta and his intentions of making war, and of my informing him that it was my intention to visit Abbeokuta in December, or early in January; after which I attacked them, and stated they were blind to certain persons, Kosoko's creatures, here, for persecuting the people of God; not allowing them their just privileges, indeed taking away their rights because they persisted in going to the church. I then told them that it was by the permission of the principal and responsible chiefs they were admitted here to teach their children and people, and of course I considered it a duty incumbent upon those said chiefs to prevent such awful persecutions by those slave-dealing villains, and I trusted and hoped that they would be able to make a good report to me, and to promise that all persecutions for the future should cease, and be prohibited by introducing a stringent law. I was sorry to state such a report would meet with the displeasure of Her Majesty's Government; such abominable proceedings. I was very anxious myself to make a good report if they would afford me the means. I then took my seat.

An aged gentleman made his appearance from the council-chamber and thanked me and the Queen of England and her Government for all the good she had done for Africa; they had not words to express their gratitude and joy for all the benefits bestowed on them by the English. It is pleasing to them when they reflect they have such a staunch friend, for they are beset by enemies on every side: there is Kosoko at Lagos, and his creatures the Jebos. They are puzzled to know why the King of Dahomey is continually troubling and threatening to destroy them for nothing; six or seven years ago he sent the late chief, Sadokee, 200 horses' tails and 40 slaves, to secure a lasting peace, but immediately after his death he turns round and threatens to exterminate us, so we are assailed on all sides. He then thanked me for taking the trouble to travel so far for the welfare of them and their children, for everything that has been done for them by the English has struck them with wonder and amazement at such overwhelming kindness; and furthermore, they hoped that God will protect me from evil, and not allow anything to molest me on my journey. He then sat down.

I arose again and thanked him kindly for his well-meant speech; I then told him that if there were any slave-dealers present, that if they had any place to get rid of their slaves besides Lagos, should there be any such characters present, I would merely impress upon their minds the dire necessity of considering in time the best method to pursue, for they may rest assured that the Queen and her Government are going at it in earnest, and are full determined to finish it at once; any number of steamers. I merely mentioned this as a friend. I then communicated my visit to Rabba several times, and Laddie (the chief, Massaba, is well known here), and of my long residence of nearly twenty-two years in Africa; that I felt a great interest in their future welfare, and should visit them again, God willing, the latter end of the year. The old gentleman made his appearance again with a short speech, then presented me with a handsome pony and a female goat, from the chiefs in general, for which I returned my most grateful thanks and sat down.

January 18. *Saturday.* 1 o'clock, the conference was opened by the war-chief Sokena. He saluted me and the missionary gentlemen, wishing us health and prosperity, thanking me for my kind visit, and begged to thank me many, many times for all I had communicated to them at the former conference on the 14th instant. The first request was to assist them in fortifying their town against the attacks of their enemies, which were at continual war with some one or other—they are the Jebos and Dahomians; secondly, relative to the Popos at Badagry, and Akitoye, the ex-King of Lagos, stating that they were forming a league with Kosoko, to take away the life of Akitoye; thirdly, they were anxious to have legitimate trade, and to do away with the foreign Slave Trade; and lastly, that they had fully determined that Akitoye should be placed under my care and protection. I told them that I would not promise anything; I would report the whole matter to the Government. As far as concerned Akitoye, I was aware he was in jeopardy; but would use my utmost endeavours, as far as an individual can be of service, to protect him from falling into the hands of the Philistines, if I arrived safe at Badagry. And as to legitimate trade, time and patience, I trusted, would ere long bring that about.

Lagos is their only sentiment: send the usurper and slave-dealers out of it, and place Akitoye in his right position; it is a grand opening, and a sweeping clause to the abominable Traffic in that quarter; the Porto Novians the same. We are not prevented by any international law that I am aware of, certainly not at Lagos; and I am not aware of any person but Domingo Martinez at Porto Novo.

The war-chiefs again desired me, on my arrival at Badagry, to use all my influence with the Popos there to deter them from entering into a league with Kosoko for the destruction of Akitoye and all his people. I promised them faithfully to use all the influence in my power, but I truly believe the Popos to be a faithless set of vagabonds. I saw through them at the conference, previous to my route here. I then asked from them a faithful promise that the persecutions against God's people should cease; they all immediately assented to it, and shook each other by the hand.

After dinner I took a short walk, and returned at sunset. 7 o'clock, Ogu-Bonno, one of the principal war-chiefs, with his two messengers that are to accompany me to Badagry, and to see me safe from the beach. Shortly afterwards, Sagbua arrived, so we retired to my private room, accompanied by Messrs Townsend, Smith, Hinderer, and Dr Van Cooten. We went over the whole of the conference, and other matters that have passed at various times relative to Akitoye and Lagos; he was now left under my protection, for they were certain that Kosoko would have his life. I harangued them strongly for not carrying out these measures at once against those persecuting wretches, instruments of that rascal at Lagos, as they please to term him. Also I told them they would allow two or three bad men to spoil their good name. Ogu-Bonno said his neck was in a noose, and in due season it should be hauled tight. They were here nearly three hours; it was a repetition of all that had passed at the different conferences. They then took their leave, and we all very readily retired to rest.

It is the current report here, that Lagos is going to war with Badagry, and is determined upon the destruction of Akitoye and Mayen; it is also reported here that Mr Hutton and another white man have been to Lagos, and that two messengers came with them from Kosoko. After family worship, retired to rest.

Consul Beecroft to Viscount Palmerston (received June 10)
Clarence, Fernando Po, February 24, 1851

My Lord,

In my previous despatch I gave your Lordship a detail of my visit to Abbeokuta, and all matters connected with Badagry, and Lagos, and Akitoye, the ex-King of Lagos. Your Lordship will find, in detail, the sentiments of the principal war-chiefs of that important place; that it is legitimate trade, and the latter place under the protection of the British flag, that would be a sweeping clause to the Slave Trade in all that vicinity; a field would be open to the interior. There are three or four large towns, within two days' journey, that are friendly to the Abbeokutians.

My Lord, I am fortunate to have escaped out of the hands of the emissaries of that vile wretch Kosoko, for it was his intention to finish my career; Mr Gollmer told me he had it from good authority; when he heard it, it was too late to write me; he had received advice of my intended departure. I can only account for the escape in having a good horse and quick travelling, performing the journey in one day less than generally done.

I have been informed by a person that was at Lagos, that the massacre in 1845 was awful; he exterminated the whole of his uncle's family and people, about 2,000, and the lagoon was a pest-house for weeks, owing to the dead carcases in it.

Commander Foote, of the "Prometheus", brought my ring that I sent by a messenger two days before I left Badagry; they met the Porto Novians on their route; they would not listen to any proposal, but sent them back with my ring. It was fortunate the "Prometheus" was off Badagry, and received a letter from Mr Gollmer, reporting the state of affairs.

Commander Foote landed an officer and men, with a field-piece; I presume it had the effect of turning the rascals back. I have not seen Commander Foote; he had left previous to the "Jackal's" arrival from Old Calabar.

The best place to land to attack Lagos is at Badagry; you go down the lagoon, *sans cérémonie*; you may surround it, being an island. My Lord, you will pardon my presuming to offer an opinion on the matter, but they all want coercion—the Porto Novians as well as others; but Lagos ought not to be allowed to escape; place the right person there, all is well. It is a well-known fact that the Slave Trade in that quarter has received a great shock.

A great number went from Abbeokuta just before I arrived. All arrived but seven; they are in great consternation.

My Lord, you are no doubt aware that the dry season is the time for Lagos; a smooth beach. I shall be enabled to communicate more fully my proceedings on my return from Benin.

JOHN BEECROFT

MARCH 1851

The Rev. H. Townsend to the Secretary of the Church Missionary Society (communicated to Viscount Palmerston by the Earl of Chichester, June 14)

Abbeokuta, Tuesday, March 4, 1851

My dear Sir,

I hasten to write a few lines, to forward to Badagry, with a hope that it may meet with an early opportunity for England.

It is with the greatest thankfulness I desire to communicate the joyful tidings of the defeat of the Dahomian King before the walls of Abbeokuta yesterday, and that they have fled, according to our latest accounts, some sixteen miles, and that the Abbeokuta people are pursuing them. The Lord has been our defender. I scarcely know how to write an account of this event, for I feel greatly agitated by the events of the past two days—a time to be ever remembered with thankfulness to Him to whom it is most justly due.

The motions of the Dahomians have been watched most thoroughly by the people of the smaller towns to the westward of this, and information sent to the chiefs here. On Saturday morning, such intelligence was conveyed as convinced the chiefs of the necessity of immediately arranging their affairs for self-defence. On Sunday, the war-chiefs formed their camps in three companies on the walls of the town. It became evident to me on Sunday evening, from the preparations which I saw going on when returning from Mr Smith's church, where I had been to assist him, and from their talk which I heard when passing, that a desperate encounter was before their minds, and that they were preparing for it with a spirit befitting the occasion.

Yesterday, Monday, I went out after breakfast, to view the camps from one of the heights. I did not direct my glass to search for the Dahomians, not knowing the road they might take, nor think of their being at hand. On returning home I heard that they had been seen, and that the advanced party of Egbas had exchanged shots with them. Mr and Mrs Smith came up to see us for a little change, having been so long ill; and Mr Dennis, who came on a visit from Badagry about a week since, also unwell, was also with us.

About 12 o'clock we heard a rapid discharge of firearms. I was in the act of showing my interpreter how to form a bullet-mould out of clay, in his house, when we heard it. With great impetuosity of manner he called for his son to bring him his gun, powder, and shot, that he might hasten to the fight, and with extreme difficulty I restrained him, he frequently exclaiming, "I cannot bear it: I must hasten to the battle." He was restrained, however. My cook, without saying anything, or our knowing of it, took his gun and ran off, and fought until the Dahomians were retreating, and shot in the fight one of the female warriors. Another confidential servant ran off in the same manner: having no arms, he proposed stoning the enemy, if they gave him an opportunity. Goodwill, who is Mr Smith's interpreter, and was left by Mr S. to look after the premises, ran also to the battle: all seemed to be beside themselves.

In order to view the encounter, Mrs Smith, Mrs Townsend, Mr Dennis, and myself, got on a high rock on our ground, whence, with a telescope, we were enabled to view it. The Dahomians advanced in compact lines or masses, bearing all before them. The Egbas endeavoured to check them at the ford of the river, but were utterly unable. They therefore retreated until withinside their walls. The walls were black with people: they poured forth their fire upon the advancing enemy, who were checked, and could not march straight on as they expected, but extended their lines in front of the wall. A most furious discharge of muskets took place from both sides. The Dahomians extended their lines, expecting to find a weak place to attack, and the Egbas extended parallel with them. At this stage of the battle I observed a large mass marching in good order to the attack, and I feared for the result; but they also extended, strengthening their companions. Mr Bowen, an American missionary, who lodges in our compound, now joined us, he having gone out long before the Dahomians appeared, to see what preparations the Egbas had made, and was on the wall at the time of the first attack. He encouraged us by his account of the firmness of the Egbas: having once been a soldier himself, he had had practical knowledge of warfare in actual service. After a time, we observed that the Dahomians showed a disposition to retire, and also that the Egbas had outflanked them, and were becoming the assailants, setting the grass on fire to annoy their enemies, and firing on them whenever they could. The Dahomians now, evidently, were retiring, but turning about constantly and discharging their muskets: they retired after awhile out of our sight, the firing becoming less and less. While this was going on, the Abbeokuta women were leaving the town at the back, pouring out before us with a few men with them, terrified and cast down: our compound was filled with terrified people. The Egbas now began to show, in truly savage style, some proofs of their success: the first was a foot of a man who had been slain, then the hand and foot of a woman, and after a while a living captive, one of the renowned women-soldiers. I followed her to the house of her captor, near my own: she was attired in a sort of vest. She spoke to me as freely as our ignorance of each other's language would admit of. The Dahomians retired to the ford.

Mr Bowen returned to the wall as a spectator, and told me that he saw a daring feat performed by a few of the Egbas. They went and provoked the Dahomians to attack them, which they did: the Egbas fled, but suddenly faced about, and discharged their guns with great effect. He thought he saw four of the Dahomians fall, but the smoke prevented distinct vision.

The Dahomians left many of their party on the battle-field dead, the greater part of whom were women, and many as prisoners, but the number we have not ascertained with any certainty. The King of Dahomey, as soon as darkness permitted, fled with 200 people, leaving the bulk of his army to cover his retreat. They were too strong to be attacked by the Egbas after a long fight, and the Egbas had too little discipline to execute an attack in the night; but they were harassed all the night through by skirmishes, and early in the morning they decamped in good order, followed by the Egbas. They stamped their character with infamy, by an act of great barbarity before retreating. They had taken a number of farmers in their march, prisoners, but before leaving they decapitated forty-two or upwards, and carried off their heads. Their hands being tied, as captives are, and many being identified by their friends, proved that they were not slain in battle: two of them were women, and one a boy. I understand that the heads were cast away in the retreat afterwards.

This King is the monster who calls himself the friend of the white people at Whydah, and of the Slave Trade, and by such wars slaves are procured! What would the members of the Peace Society have done behind the walls of Abbeokuta, with these disciplined barbarians advancing in masses to the attack? Through mercy they have been repelled, but many of the Egbas have fallen, and many are severely wounded.

One of my candidates came to us in the afternoon, begging for some one to extract a shot from his shoulder: it had entered at the side of the upper part of the arm, and passed about six inches through the flesh, outside of the shoulder-blade. Mr Dennis ventured to try, although he had never done anything of the sort before, and after considerable trouble cut it out. The poor man's first act, on hearing that it was out, was to bring himself into an attitude of prayer; and silently he offered up thanks to God for His mercy. He is doing well.

It is supposed that 200 or 300 of the Dahomians are lying dead on the battle-field, and many have been captured. They are retreating in a compact body, but in great distress. If they had broken in their retreat, scarcely a man or woman could have escaped the Egbas to-day. They are still being pursued, but a large number of the Egbas have returned, worn out by their two days' exertions. I feel also worn out by excitement, and by witnessing and hearing of so much slaughter and cruelty. I am not aware that the Egbas have acted cruelly towards their prisoners.

Wednesday, March 5

Several persons have returned from the pursuit this morning, bringing the intelligence of a desperate encounter at a town called Ishaga, about fourteen or sixteen miles from this. The Dahomians endeavoured to enter this town, for rest or pillage, but were resisted. The Egbas came up with a strong force at the time, and the Dahomians were again driven, and, I understand, divided. It is said that a part of the personal luggage and provisions of the King fell into their hands, and that he was obliged to fly on foot. The number slain in this battle was more, they say, than those before Abbeokuta. The Egbas could not make captives in this battle: even when disarmed, they (the Dahomians) fought and refused to surrender, and they were killed.

I am sorry to report that one of Mr Crowther's communicants is missing, but he may yet be found. In order to find him, if he were among the slain, Mr C. passed over the greater part of the battle-field, and his report of the number slain is such as to give a greater number. He says they are lying in fours and fives, in various directions, over a large extent of ground. The length of wall attacked was upwards of a mile.

I sent two persons out this morning to count the slain Dahomians: one counted them in tens, and the other wrote the number down—and, to our surprise, it amounts to 1,209. It confirms the report brought to us by a deserter, an Egba man who had long been a Dahomian slave, that the Dahomians, when gathered together at night, were struck dumb at the loss they had sustained, especially of their female soldiers, and only one thing was uttered by all—viz., a fear that they would never be able to return home.

This is a slave war, and we might justly ask, for what were all these slain? To supply the slave-market with slaves! would be a just reply. The people everywhere here seem to ascribe their deliverance to God and the white men. I hope the Dahomian King will learn a lesson from this, and cease from these barbarous wars, for which not the shadow of a cause was given by the Egbas, nor, I suppose, by most of the other towns that he has warred against. It is to be hoped that the Egbas will not become too boastful of their victory, and be led into excesses. I fear it, but it is a satisfaction to know that our gracious Saviour and God is over us, to protect from moral as well physical evils, and will not suffer His cause to be uprooted.

I hope you will excuse this hasty letter, but I could not let an opportunity slip, or the probability of one, knowing that you would be anxious on our account, more especially as false rumours may reach you by other channels than those available to us. With much thankfulness to God, and desire for your prayers and sympathy for this unhappy country.

H. TOWNSEND

P.S. I can form no estimate of the number of prisoners, or of the Dahomian army. I asked a captive how many retired with the King, when they felt themselves defeated, to be out of danger. He said 200. I asked again, how many were there in the army? He said that even as it was impossible for me to count the people of Abbeokuta, so was it for me to count their army.

The Dahomian captives are desperate: there are three several instances of their rising against their captors and slaying them in their own houses—one when he was in the act of giving his captive food. The people treat their prisoners kindly, but I fear all these will be killed, unless we can prevent it by any means. I was with Sagbua this morning, and the subject was discussed. I protested against it. A meeting was proposed, and I told him that they ought not to have a meeting without calling me to it. The prisoners are, however, private property, and this may hinder their being killed. I feel assured that the Egbas would exchange a captive for an Egba slave now in the Dahomian Country.

March 6, 1851

Commodore Fanshawe to the Secretary of the Admiralty
"Centaur", off Quittah, March 25, 1851

Sir,

With reference to my despatch to you of the 28th October, 1850, when his Lordship considered it important I should ascertain if the letter I had addressed to the King of Dahomey on the subject of his making war on Abbeokuta, had been received by His Majesty; I have the honour to request you will be pleased to acquaint their Lordships that I have ascertained that the letter was received by the King, and that he very quickly sent down messengers from Abomey to Whydah with the letter, and instructions to his Cabooceer at the latter place to request (through the agent of Mr Hutton) that the senior officer of Her Majesty's ships would send an officer on shore to explain the contents of the letter, as he "wished no Portuguese to hear of any of his affairs with the Englishmen".

The attention of Captain Adams being occupied at the moment with some disturbances in the Benin and Calabar Rivers, affecting British property, some time elapsed before he was able to comply with this request, but on his return to Whydah he sent Lieutenant Dew, Senior Lieutenant of the "Gladiator", on shore for the pupose; and I enclose a copy of his report to Captain Adams on return, of his interview with the Cabooceer, and of an extract from Captain Adams' general report to me on rejoining him, which I hope will be satisfactory to their Lordships and Her Majesty's Government; both as showing the respect of the King of Dahomey for Her

Majesty and her subjects, and the general depression of the Slave Trade in this quarter.

The King I understand to be now occupied on a slave-hunt; but I am proceeding to Badagry, where I may perhaps receive further intelligence of him.

ARTHUR FANSHAWE

Enclosure 1

Lieutenant Dew to Captain Adams
"Gladiator", off Whydah, February 27, 1851

Sir,

In obedience to your order, I landed at Whydah on the 26th instant, and was received on the beach by Mr Reynolds, an agent of Mr Hutton's; he provided hammocks, and we were carried to the town, distant four miles. I immediately proceeded to the residence of the Cabooceer, accompanied by Mr Reynolds, who acted as interpreter, and was received by him and his headmen. A letter was put into my hands, written by Commodore Fanshawe, and addressed to the King of Dahomey, which the Cabooceer requested me to read: I did so, explaining it paragraph by paragraph to him and his chiefs, no white person being present.

He stated that this letter had been to Abomey, but the King would not permit it to be read by the Portuguese resident there, as it might affect their interests.

The Cabooceer stated, on the part of the King of Dahomey, that it was not his intention to make war on Abbeokuta, and that all British subjects in his dominions should be held sacred.

He stated it was his wish to stop the Slave Trade, but as all his revenue was derived from it he must have compensation. He wished the Queen of England to send some officer on revenue days to see the amount he received from the

Slave Traffic, so that she may judge what she ought to give him to stop the Trade. He would stop it in all parts of his dominions, save Whydah, but there he could not stop it at present, as there were too many Portuguese residing there, who paid him the greater part of his revenue.

Mr Reynolds told me that the Slave Trade was in a most depressed state, no shipment having taken place for many months, and that the slave-merchants finding all efforts to get off slaves futile, had commenced trafficking in palm-oil. M. da Souza was then loading two vessels in the roads.

In consequence of the heavy surf, no canoe-men could be induced to bring me off last night, and it was only by using threats this morning that I obtained a canoe. Since the death of Mr Hastie, the King of Dahomey has threatened death to any canoe-men who may lose the life of any Englishman, and I attribute the difficulty of obtaining a boat to this, and to no other cause.

R. Dew

Enclosure 2

Captain Adams to Commodore Fanshawe

(Extract)   *"Gladiator", March* 24, 1851

Every assistance has been rendered to the British missionaries at Badagry, agreeably to your directions, keeping up a repeated communication with that place, and exercising at general quarters in this ship and in the several cruizers in that part of the Bights.

I continue to receive repeated assurances from the most credible persons, of the decline of the Slave Trade on this part of the coast, owing, as it is alleged, to the strict blockade maintained by Her Majesty's cruizers here.

The British missionaries at Abbeokuta and at Badagry acquaint me that the Traffic from Cape St Paul to Lagos is nearly at an end; that within the last two months 135 slaves were marched down from Abbeokuta to Lagos, for sale to the slave-merchants, but they were unable to find a purchaser. Five of them were afterwards sold as domestic slaves, the rest were marched back into the interior; a circumstance hitherto unheard of by any of the residents. They further allege that many of the slave-dealers are ruined, and that at Lagos some of them are actually selling the furniture out of their houses to procure provisions for their slaves.

The French merchant-barque "Tourville" touched at Fernando Po. She was bound to London with a cargo of palm-oil from Don Jozé Domingo Martinez, consigned to Messrs Forster and Smith. The supercargo informed me that he was at Porto Novo three months shipping his cargo; and from Don Martinez' remarks, and his own observation, he considered the Traffic thereabouts nearly at an end.

Martinez asserted that if the British took or destroyed Lagos, Slavery would be done away with in the Bights. That he was present when Martinez refused to purchase slaves at from 7 to 8 dollars each, stating he had come to the determination of having no more to do with them, owing to the difficulties of the passage across to Brazil. That Martinez realized large sums by the trade in palm-oil.

The deposed King of Lagos with some of his family and retinue were brought from Badagry to Fernando Po in the "Jackal", by Her Majesty's Consul, a reward having been offered for his head by the present usurper.

Commodore Fanshawe to the Secretary of the Admiralty
"Centaur", off the River Benin, March 30, 1851

Sir,

In my despatch of the 25th instant, from Quittah, I expressed my intention of proceeding to Badagry, with the expectation of obtaining further information of the movements of the King of Dahomey; and I have now to request that you will be pleased to lay before the Lords Commissioners of the Admiralty copies of letters which I received on my arrival off Badagry on the 26th instant, from the Church missionaries at that place and at Abbeokuta, giving me the account of a furious assault which the King with his army had made on Abbeokuta on the 3rd instant; and, I am happy to add, of the signal repulse and defeat which he experienced.

This attack and conduct is quite irreconcilable with the assurance which had so recently been given to Lieutenant Dew, of the "Gladiator", by the Cabooceer at Whydah, of the King's intentions, and with the promised protection for British subjects throughout his dominions, made at a moment when one must suppose he knew his master was actually marching on Abbeokuta.

I therefore must conceive him guilty of the basest deceit and false-hood, or otherwise attribute it to the King having found himself obliged, for his own security, to yield to the repeated demands of the army to be led against the Egbas, backed by the Intagees, and promised assistance of Kosoko, the usurping King of Lagos, who appears to have been much incensed at his rival and kinsman, the ex-King Akitoye, having been taken by Her Majesty's Consul, Mr Beecroft, on his return from Abbeokuta, in January, from Badagry to Fernando Po, under, as he supposed, British protection.

Learning that Mr Beecroft was detained in the Benin, I proceeded, without delay, from Badagry to this anchorage, for the purpose of conferring with him as to the course it might be desirable to adopt; and I have to request you will be pleased to inform their Lordships, that after full consideration with him to-day of all the circumstances with which we are at present acquainted, I have decided that, unless actual outrage or injury to a British subject should occur, it will be more prudent not to follow up my intention of stopping the trade at Whydah and coast contiguous, by the declaration of a blockade of the Dahomian territory, but to submit the subject for the consideration of Her Majesty's Government.

I beg at the same time you will assure their Lordships, that this determination has not arisen from any desire to shrink from the responsibility of such a course, as it might regard other Powers, but solely from the apprehension that any premature act might place the lives of the missionaries and their adherents in great danger, whilst it would not be known in time to influence the further warlike measures of the King this season, and would entirely preclude the placing Her Majesty's Vice-Consul at Whydah, whom I had brought on in this ship to join Mr Beecroft. And, I have also learnt from Captain Adams, who has joined me at this anchorage, that on his hearing, off Whydah, of this assault on Abbeokuta, he had sent on shore a letter to the King, representing again the consequence of any injury being sustained by Her Majesty's subjects.

I cannot close this despatch without respectfully calling the attention of their Lordships to the fact, which will indeed, perhaps, strike them as forcibly as it has done me, viz., how impossible it is to place any reliance on the information Her Majesty's officers receive from the Agent at Whydah of Messrs Hutton, I believe the only British mercantile firm in the Kingdom of Dahomey. He appears to have been chosen as the organ of communication between the Cabooceer and Lieutenant Dew, and almost to have been a party to the deceit which was practised; and therefore how desirable it is that the old British Fort at Whydah should be occupied by some one holding authority under Her Majesty.

ARTHUR FANSHAWE

JULY 1851

Commodore Bruce to the Secretary of the Admiralty
"Penelope", Ascension, July 3, 1851

Sir,

I request you will lay before the Lords Commissioners of the Admiralty the accompanying extract of a letter of proceedings from Commander J. N. Strange, of Her Majesty's steam-sloop "Archer", with its enclosure, being a communication from Guezo, the King of Dahomey.

Their Lordships will observe from the report of Commander Strange, which is confirmed by all the information I have received on the subject, that the war between the Dahomians and the Yoruba tribes has been most disastrous to the former. I have therefore deemed it right to entertain the King's request for an officer to be sent to him, because I think it is not improbable that he may now agree to an anti-Slave Trade Treaty with Great Britain; and I have accordingly directed Commander A. P. E. Wilmot, of the "Harlequin", to accompany Mr Beecroft, Her Majesty's Consul in the Bights of Benin and Biafra, to the town of Abomey, and enter into a negotiation on the terms laid down in Viscount Palmerston's despatch to Mr Beecroft dated February 25, 1850.

I also enclose copies of my letters to King Guezo, Commander Wilmot, and Mr Beecroft.

H. W. Bruce

Enclosure 1

Commander Strange to Commodore Fanshawe

(Extract)   *"Archer", Ascension, June* 25, 1851

With regard to the Dahomey War, I am informed by Mr Gollmer, that there appears to be no immediate prospect of a renewal of hostilities, and that the estimated loss of the King of Dahomey is 16,000 killed and taken prisoners. Domingo Martinez has been employed lately in purchasing the prisoners from both parties, professedly for the purpose of effecting exchanges and bringing about peace.

I have the honour to enclose a copy of a document (the original of which was received by Commander Patey, and is now in Captain Jones' hands) in which the King of Dahomey expresses a wish that Her Majesty would send some person to hold a palaver with him. The Vice-Consul had not arrived at Whydah, and I had no opportunity of sending the document to Mr Beecroft.

Enclosure 2
The King of Dahomey to Her Majesty Queen Victoria

To Her Most Gracious Majesty Victoria, Queen of
England, Defender of the Faith, etc.

The King of Dahomey sends his compliments to Her
Majesty, greeting, and wishes she would send him, as he
expresses it, a soldier with a good head to hear some palaver
from his mouth at the town of Abomey, so that he may
report the same to Her Majesty.

For GUEZO
King of the Country of Dahomey

(Signed) GEORGE PRIOR

Given through Madaki, as interpreter.

Enclosure 3
Commodore Bruce to the King of Dahomey
"Penelope," June 28, 1851

As the Commander-in-Chief of the Fleet of Her Majesty
the Queen of England in these seas, I have received your
Majesty's note, wherein you request that a soldier with a
good head may be sent to hear some palaver from your
mouth at the town of Abomey; and in compliance with
your desire, I have made arrangements for John Beecroft,
Esq., Her Majesty's Consul, and Commander A. P. E.
Wilmot, of the ship of war "Harlequin", to visit you and
learn your wishes.

Your Majesty will remember, that some time since, the
former gentleman, accompanied by Lieutenant Forbes, had
several interviews with you at Abomey; and, amongst other
things, pointed out that the Slave Trade would be done
away with before long. Notwithstanding this, your Majesty
declined to assist the Queen of England in the immediate

suppression of that cruel Traffic, by signing a Treaty to this effect: late events will have proved to you the truth of their assertion. You must know that the Traffic in question is all but annihilated, in consequence of the vigorous measures adopted by the English and other civilized Governments, and which measures will never be relaxed until the object for which they were commenced has been effected. I trust that a few months' reflection has convinced your Majesty that your true and permanent interests are identical with the establishment of legal commerce; and that the liberal allowance which the Queen of England would make to you for a series of years, combined with that commerce, is better worth your consideration than the uncertain and decreasing revenue you may derive from foreign slave-dealers.

I hope to hear of peace having been concluded between your Majesty and the people of Abbeokuta. And I must take this opportunity of reminding you of the tenor of the note addressed to you by Commodore Fanshawe (who has returned to England), that the Queen my Sovereign would be very much displeased with, and would certainly punish, any one who molested the persons or violated the property of any of her subjects located in your Majesty's dominions or elsewhere.

I recommend to your Majesty's especial care the distinguished gentlemen who are the bearers of this despatch: one of them you know already, as a person of high rank and consideration in the civil service of the Queen of England; the other is a distinguished officer in command of a ship of war. I am confident you will communicate freely with them, and extend to them that friendship and hospitality for which your Majesty is so much esteemed.

HENRY W. BRUCE

Enclosure 4

Commodore Bruce to Commander Wilmot
"Penelope", Ascension, June 28, 1851

Sir,

You are probably aware that it has long been the desire of
Her Majesty's Government to enter into a Treaty with the
King of Dahomey for the suppression of the foreign Slave
Trade, which is carried on to a great extent in his dominions; and that, with this view, Mr Consul Beecroft, and
Lieutenant Forbes of the "Bonetta", were dispatched to the
town of Abomey in May 1850. They, however, failed in the
object of their mission, the King urging, that from the Slave
Trade alone could he expect to receive a certain and sufficient revenue for the requirements of his kingdom. Since
that period the condition of Dahomey has materially
changed: a disastrous war with the neighbouring tribes in
the Yoruba Country, and the virtual cessation of the Traffic,
on which the King depended for support, must have
impoverished the chiefs and humbled their spirits. It would
therefore appear to be a desirable moment for us to renew
our efforts to induce the King to engage never again to
permit slaves to be exported from his territory to countries
beyond the sea.

It happened, very opportunely, that I have received
a paper from the King of Dahomey, in which he expressed
a wish that Her Majesty would send to him "a soldier with a
good head to hear some palaver". It may be that the King's
object is merely to have some influential mediator between
him and the people of Yoruba; but, at all events, advantage
may be taken of his request to further the views of Her
Majesty's Government, which, as well as the extinction of
the Slave Trade, desires the termination of a war that
involves the personal security of the British residents,
missionaries, and others located at Abbeokuta and in its
vicinity.

Having entire confidence in your zeal and judgement, and hearing that you are desirous of undertaking the expedition, I have selected you to perform the important service of proceeding, in company with Mr Beecroft, to the town of Abomey, where you will find the King of Dahomey, and deliver to him the enclosed letter.

On being introduced to the King, you will acquaint him that I, as the Commander-in-Chief of Her Majesty's Fleet in these seas, have received his note, requesting that an officer may be sent to him "to hear some palaver", that I have acceded to his request, because, notwithstanding his former refusal to enter into a treaty, and thereby declining, as it were, the friendship of the Queen of England, I believe that Her Majesty would be graciously pleased to forgive what has passed on hearing that he (the King) now entertains the propositions of her Government with respect to the Slave Trade.

The despatch from the Right Honourable Viscount Palmerston to John Beecroft, Esquire (a copy of which is annexed, for your information and guidance), dated the 25th February, 1850, will furnish you with arguments proper to be used in your interviews with the King; I can add nothing to them beyond what is suggested from the different aspect of affairs in Dahomey since that despatch was written. I desire you to make known to the King, that the British Government is fully determined to stop the Traffic in Slaves, and that good policy alone should induce him to assist in this object, as there is no doubt, in a very short time, it will be accomplished without his assistance. You will acquaint him that the ships of England are blockading the coasts of the countries to which his slaves are exported; that the rulers of those countries are resolved to prevent the people from continuing to bring over slaves; that the dealers are expelled and ruined; that all civilized Governments are now ranged on our side; and that in a few months the Slave Trade must cease for ever. In support of this it would be well to draw his attention to the diminution in the Traffic of late; and, in conclusion, put it to him, whether a liberal and certain stipend from Great Britain, for three years, in addition to the revenue which he might obtain from the productions of his rich country and the establishment of legal commerce, would not be more advantageous to him, than obstinately clinging to a course which will ultimately leave him in poverty, and without a friend.

With regard to the war between Dahomey and the Yoruba tribes, you will, if requested to do so by the King, use your influence to bring about a peace, more particularly if the Dahomians should agree to an anti-Slave Trade Treaty, or are likely to get the better of the struggle in the end; but if, on the contrary, they should refuse to negotiate on the terms proposed, and you think it probable that the Yoruba tribes will conquer, you will acquaint the King that you are not authorized to interfere against the interests of those people, because they are assisting us in the suppression of the Slave Trade. In either case you will make the King distinctly understand, that if any British subjects suffer in life or property through his measures, the Queen of England will hold him responsible.

I need scarcely remind you, that in order to ensure the success of your mission, it is necessary that the most cordial understanding should exist between you and your colleague, Mr Beecroft. You will find him to be a very intelligent gentleman, possessing great local knowledge, and having considerable influence with the native chiefs and people. I request you will attend to such suggestions as he, in his position as Her Majesty's Consul and Diplomatic Agent, may make to you. You will communicate these instructions to him, and I shall request him to make you acquainted with the tenor of the despatches and orders he may have received from the Queen's Government with respect to Dahomey.

As soon as you are joined by Mr Beecroft, and he is ready to accompany you, you will proceed in execution of this service, and make a full report to me of every particular connected with it as early as possible after your return to the "Harlequin".

Many weeks may have transpired since Guezo's note was written, and much time may elapse before Mr Beecroft is able to reach Whydah; in the interim, the political condition of Dahomey will perhaps have changed; I have therefore left it to his judgement whether or not to accede to the King's request, and you are to be governed by his decision in this respect.

H.W. BRUCE

Enclosure 5
Commodore Bruce to Consul Beecroft
"Penelope", Ascension, June 28, 1851

Sir,

I do myself the honour to enclose a copy of a communication transmitted to me from Guezo, King of Dahomey, by which you will perceive that he is anxious for an interview with a British officer.

It appears to me that the reverses this chief has met with in the war between him and the Yoruba tribes, added to the diminution, I may almost say complete cessation, of the Slave Trade on the sea-coast of his dominions, may be taken advantage of by us to urge on him the expediency of entering into an anti-Slave Trade Treaty with Great Britain, according to the form supplied to you by the Right Honourable Viscount Palmerston, and on the conditions expressed in his Lordship's despatch dated the 25th of February, 1850.

I am of opinion that as soon as you have completed the service at Lagos, which forms the subject of my letter dated the 31st of May last, you would do well to proceed to the town of Abomey, and renew an intercourse with King Guezo, with a view to induce him to negotiate on the terms proposed when you last visited his capital.

On the supposition that you will undertake this duty, I have directed Commander A. P. E. Wilmot, of Her Majesty's ship "Harlequin", to place himself in communication with you, and accompany you to Abomey. A copy of my instructions to him I enclose herewith for your information.

Many weeks may have transpired since Guezo's note was written, and much time may elapse before you are able to reach Whydah; in the interim, the political condition of Dahomey may have changed; I must therefore leave it to your judgement whether or not to accede to the King's request, and Commander Wilmot will be governed by your decision.

H. W. BRUCE

Commodore Bruce to the Secretary of the Admiralty
"Penelope", Prince's Island, July 31, 1851

Sir,

I have the honour to transmit herewith, for the information of the Lords Commissioners of the Admiralty, copies of correspondence relating to an attack lately made on Badagry by the people of Lagos.

Independent of the desire which I entertain of carrying out the instructions of Her Majesty's Government to protect the missionaries and other British subjects residing at the former place, I should be glad of an opportunity to punish the present King and chiefs of Lagos, who pertinaciously adhere to the Slave Trade, and resist all our efforts to induce them to enter into a Treaty for the abolition of the same; but in the present instance, as far as matters have yet gone, I think their Lordships will see that the quarrel between Badagry and Lagos is purely of a domestic nature, and not one which warrants a neutral Power to interfere in a hostile manner. If, for instance, the murder of Gee and the Krooman in the employ of Mr Batten, had been proved to have been committed by Lagos people, I should, failing in obtaining redress, have deemed it my duty to attack the town and blockade the coast; but the evidence necessary to authorize such proceedings is not sufficiently clear; and indeed, from the statements of Captain Jones and Commander Heath, I am inclined to believe that it was the work of some men belonging to Badagry.

I trust their Lordships will approve of Commander Heath having declined to accede to the request of the British residents at Badagry to land an armed force there from Her Majesty's steam-sloop "Niger". In the first place, the climate, particularly at this season, is most destructive to the lives of Europeans; in the next, the number of men he could have landed would have been so few, in proportion to the number they might have been called upon to engage, that the issue would have been doubtful; added to which, no provisions could be obtained from the shore, and the surf frequently prevents all communication with ships.

To ensure the protection of British life and property, I have directed Captain Jones, the senior officer in the Bights Division, to continue to keep a vessel of war stationed off Badagry, with instructions for her commander to communicate with the missionaries and others as frequently as the state of the beach will admit; and on their requesting it, to receive them on board, with as much of their property as can possibly be got off; and should a case come to his knowledge where British life has been wantonly sacrificed, or British property wilfully destroyed by either of the contending parties, to acquaint me with the particulars forthwith, and in the meantime to take such defensive measures as the circumstances may appear to require.

I have also written letters to the King of Lagos and the Chief of Porto Novo, warning them against molesting British subjects.

H.W. BRUCE

Enclosure 1

Commander Heath to Commodore Bruce
"Niger", Badagry, June 20, 1851

Sir,

I have the honour to inform you, that on the morning of the 14th instant, whilst at anchor off Porto Novo, I received information of a revolution having taken place at Badagry, and of the native town having been burnt down.

I immediately weighed and ran down, and shortly after anchoring, was visited by Mr Duggan, supercargo of the "Severn", who professed himself perfectly acquainted with the state of affairs, and with the feelings of the missionary (Mr Gollmer) and the other European residents. He described the fight which had taken place on the 12th instant as being a purely native quarrel, with which the English had nothing to do, and by which the English were not likely to be injured, except inasmuch as it would stop the trade for a time. A small portion of English property had, he said, been accidentally burnt during the general conflagration of the town.

Letters passed between the English residents and myself on the 17th instant. At 4 PM on the 18th, the English ensigns on shore were all hoisted, union down; I therefore, in accordance with the signal agreed upon, sent boats to the back of the surf, but seeing no indications of any embarkation, I thought it best to land myself and ascertain what was going on. On landing I met a messenger and I immediately proceeded to the mission-house, and had an interview with Messrs Gollmer, Sandeman, McCaskey, and Martin. These gentleman again urged me to land men for their protection, which I again refused, on the ground that there could be no danger to their lives if they would adopt my suggestion of removing either to the beach or to the ships, and that I thought it better there should be a probable loss of some of their property, than a certain loss by fever of a great portion of the men I might land. I also informed them that I was acting in accordance with verbal orders I had received from Commodore Fanshawe. I then inquired if there was any other way except that of landing men, in which I could assist them, and they suggested that a letter to the King of Lagos might perhaps induce him to issue orders that in the event of his people retaking Badagry, English life and property should be secured and respected.

When on the point of returning on board, I heard that a large body of warriors from Abbeokuta were on their march to assist that party which is now dominant, and which has hitherto so carefully respected British property. I am therefore under no apprehension of any danger to the English at present.

It is difficult to unravel all the intricacies of an African quarrel, but from a comparison of the information I have received from various quarters, I have concluded that the following is not far from a true statement of the case.

About six years ago, Akitoye, the King of Lagos, was expelled from his throne by Kosoko, the present King. Akitoye, with his followers, took refuge in Badagry which was then inhabited by a race called Popos. Jealousy and party spirit soon arose, and a feud commenced between Akitoye's followers and the Popos, who sided with Kosoko. The principal cause of this, as far as I can understand was, that the Popos had been accustomed to have an uninterrupted canoe-communication all along the lagoon from Porto Novo to Lagos, which Akitoye's party, being hostile to Lagos, wished to intercept at Badagry.

On Thursday the 12th instant a large body of Lagos people came up the lagoon and landed at Badagry, visiting and doing business with their friends the Popos. Whilst in the market-place some of them sang songs, the burden of which was abuse and insult to Akitoye. Akitoye's party seized and chained two of the culprits. The Lagos people and Popos flew to arms; the fight commenced, and the town was burnt to the ground. The victory remained completely in the hands of Akitoye's party, whose chief is a respectable man called Mayen.

So much for that which is past. As for the future, it is supposed that the Porto Novo people will endeavour to avenge the defeat of their friends; whilst on the other hand, a large body of Abbeokutians is actually on its march for the defence of the present rulers of Badagry.

There is no doubt that we have not hitherto maintained a strict neutrality between the two parties. Mr Beecroft, the Consul-General, carried Akitoye as a sort of protégé to Fernando Po, and Mr Gollmer himself told me in the course of conversation two or three weeks before these disturbances, that Akitoye's people came to him for advice, saying, "Now Akitoye is gone we look to you as our head, he left us to your care when he went"; so that if the tables are turned, and the Popos victorious, our countrymen will no longer be as safe as at present.

L.G. HEATH

Enclosure 2
The British residents at Badagry to Commander Heath
[*June* 18, 1851]

Sir,

We have the honour to acknowledge the receipt of your two letters of yesterday, the latter accompanied by 3,000 ball-cartridges, conveying to us that you must decline acceding to our request to land men for our protection; and suggesting that we with our property should remove either on board the vessels in port, or down to the beach, within reach of the ship's guns; also that you must adhere to your resolution not to land men.

In reply we beg to say that communications from Commodore Fanshawe, Captain Adams, Captain Strange, Captain Patey, and Captain Foote, repeatedly assured us of their readiness to render us any assistance in their power, not only to take us on board of Her Majesty's ships, but land men to protect our lives and property on shore.

Accordingly we yesterday requested you to afford us the protection we so much need in our present critical position, and were not a little disappointed at the non-compliance of our request.

With regard to your suggestion to remove our property to the beach, and embarking or removing to Mr Batten's house, the utter impracticability of following either of your suggestions we should have thought to be quite apparent, when it was stated that one merchant alone had between 4,000*l.* and 5,000*l.* on shore; besides we cannot get a single man to work, and were we to attempt embarking it would cause a panic, and the canoe-men would look after themselves; and so far from considering ourselves or property safer on the beach with nothing but the ship's guns to protect us, we consider both ourselves and it safer where we are: nor can we think for a moment of running away and leaving property committed to our charge while a chance remains of saving it; neither do we think you would recommend such a course, on consideration.

The commanders of Her Majesty's ships of war do not generally pay so much consideration to the health of their crews when a slaver is in the question, and surely the protection of sixteen or eighteen Englishmen, with a large amount of property, besides some hundreds of British subjects (liberated Africans), who in case of defeat would most assuredly be again consigned to Slavery, is a matter of at least not less importance.

We enclose the receipt for the cartridges you kindly sent us, and for which we return our sincere thanks.

C.A. GOLLMER *et al.*

Enclosure 3
Commander Heath to the British residents at Badagry
"Niger", Badagry, June 19, 1851

Gentlemen,

Although I have had a verbal communication with you since the receipt on the 18th instant of your letter (without date), I think it right to point out officially how very unnecessary and uncalled for is the last paragraph in that letter.

However much we may differ in opinion as to the proper method of meeting the present crisis in your affairs, there is no reason why our correspondence should become acrimonious, and I therefore hope that on consideration you will withdraw the words I complain of, viz.,

"The Commanders of Her Majesty's ships of war do not generally pay so much consideration to the health of their crews when a slaver is in the question."

L.G. HEATH

Enclosure 4
Captain Jones to Kosoko, Chief of Lagos

I have heard with deep regret of the disturbances that have taken place at Badagry, in a quarrel between the people of Lagos and the people of Badagry, in consequence of which the usually quiet and well-conducted trade between the British merchants and the people of the country has been disturbed, and much native property destroyed.

The English came here for purposes of trade, and are anxious to keep clear of all international quarrels, and they are sorry that there should be any disturbance amongst the natives. Mayen's party are now victorious, and Mayen has taken very great trouble to protect the English and their property.

Captain Jones hopes there will be no more war, but that both parties will now make peace. Should, however, the contrary be the case, and the Lagos people gain the day, he hopes and thinks, from what Kosoko knows of the power and strength of the English nation, he will give orders to respect the houses where the English flag, which he so well knows, is flying.

Given under my hand, this 20th day of June, 1851.

LEWIS T. JONES

Enclosure 5
Commander Heath to Commodore Bruce
"Niger", Badagry, July 17, 1851

Sir,

In continuation of my last report of proceedings dated June 20th, I have the honour to inform you that on the 27th June I landed and had an interview with Mayen, the Governor of Badagry, and Shamyei, the commander of an auxiliary force of two or three thousand men sent from Abbeokuta. My intention was merely to thank them for the protection afforded by them to my countrymen, and to request a continuance of the same conduct; but Shamyei took the opportunity of giving me the whole history of the war, ending his story with an earnest request that Akitoye might be brought back from Fernando Po, and set up by us as King of Lagos; "then," he said, "there would be no more wars in this country." I replied that what he asked was quite out of my power, but that I would report all he had said to you. I need not give you a more detailed account of his speech, as I observe that he (or more probably the missionary in his name) has sent a similar statement in writing to the senior officer.

On endeavouring to return to the ship the canoe upset, and I regret to say Mr Duffus, the assistant surgeon (who had landed with me in compliance with a requisition from the shore for medical assistance to the wounded), was drowned, whilst I but very narrowly escaped the same fate.

It is supposed that the King of Porto Novo will join his forces to those of Lagos, and thus place Badagry between two fires. I therefore proceeded on the 30th June to Porto Novo, and sent a letter to the King, through Don Domingo.

A few cases of fever, one of them fatal, having broken out whilst at anchor off Badagry (where I am obliged to lay close in, that the guns may command the lagoon, if necessary). I worked to windward for four days, partly for the sake of change of air, and partly in hopes of falling in with and reporting the progress of affairs to Captain Jones; but not meeting the "Sampson", I returned on the 5th July to Badagry, and then heard that on the evening of the 2nd an English carpenter and Krooman in the employ of Mr Batten, had been shot dead on the beach. Mr Batten holds the opinion that this act was committed by Lagos people, but I have heard from two other sources that they were idle Badagrians, and I am inclined to think this the most probable account.

Since then nothing of importance has occurred. Her Majesty's ship "Prometheus" has been here, and Captain Foote has taken the senior officer's letter to Kosoko, and intends, I believe, to obtain, if possible, a personal interview, in order to impress the contents of the letter more forcibly upon him.

L.G. HEATH

Enclosure 6

Commander Heath to the King of Porto Novo

In the late disturbances at Badagry, it appears that the party of Mayen and Akitoye has gained the victory, and driven out the friends of the King of Porto Novo.

In all these disturbances, Mayen has most strictly and honourably protected the English and their property.

What I now ask is, that the King of Porto Novo will promise me, on the faith of a King, that in any expedition he may send to revenge his cause at Badagry, he will give strict orders to protect the English and their property as carefully as the other party have hitherto done.

The English do not wish to take any part in the quarrels of the country; let the natives fight as much as they choose, but let them beware if an Englishman suffers.

Given under my hand, this 29th day of June, 1851

L.G. HEATH

AUGUST–SEPTEMBER 1851

The Rev. H. Townsend to Commander Wilmot
(Extract)   *Abbeokuta, August* 5, 1851
Having a common interest in the welfare of Badagry and
the English residing there, the English residents at
Abbeokuta have heard with some concern, that you are
unable to render such assistance as would enable Her
Britannic Majesty's subjects to maintain their position, and
that nothing is left them but either to abandon it, or
depend on their own or native aid for preservation. It is a
painful position to be placed in, but while it arises out of
circumstances over which they have no control, they may
with more certainty make use of such means as are given
for self-preservation, trusting in a Divine Providence which
is ever extended over those that most need it.

I would not trouble you with this letter, for which I have to apologize, but from observing in a copy of the letter addressed to the King of Porto Novo the following remark: "The English do not wish to take part in the quarrel of the country; let the nations fight as long as they choose, but let them beware if an Englishman suffers." I would gather from this passage, and from one in a letter from Captain Jones, who calls the native wars a "native squabble", that Her Majesty's officers regard the war at Badagry as having no reference to the English or the acts of the British Government; but allow me with much deference to remark, that these wars result from the acts of Her Majesty's cruizers, and from the efforts of Englishmen towards establishing lawful trade. And I would further remark that they are directed against the English nationally, and not the English individually.

Obba Shoron to Commander Wilmot
Badagry, September 3, 1851

Sir,

I, Obba Shoron, second to the King, and Commander-in-Chief of the forces of all Abbeokuta, salute you and wish you long life.

I was glad to see your face and tell you what is in my heart; however, I thought I must put my words on paper, that you may not forget them.

I and my people are the Egba tribe of the Yoruba nation. Our fathers were farmers and lived peaceably in many towns, but war broke their towns and drove them from their homes; and so they and we, their children, built all at one place, that is Abbeokuta, which is now a large town with more than 80,000 people.

We all are farmers and traders, and do not wish for war, but we have many enemies, and to defend ourselves we must fight.

Dahomey is our enemy. We have done him no wrong, but he is jealous of our large town, and thinks we shall get too strong, and so he came with a large army in the beginning of the year to destroy our town and make slaves of us, but we defeated him; and now he promises to try again in about four months.

Kosoko at Lagos is our enemy, because we are more friendly to the English than to Portuguese. We did not drive the English from our town as he wished us to do, but seek still more friendship and trade with English. He is our enemy, because we are Akitoye's friends. Kosoko spends much money all about to set the people against us, and so to defend ourselves we are obliged to engage in war.

Kosoko is the cause of war at Badagry. He bribed the Popos to kill and to catch Akitoye's people and to drive (or kill) the English from this place, but the Popos lost the war. Kosoko long desired to shut the road between Badagry and Abbeokuta, that we should not be able to trade with the English any more; and therefore as soon as we heard of the war here, and that this town, our only port, will be spoiled, I came down with the people to help in defending the town against Kosoko, who sent many large canoes with many people and big guns in them, to destroy this place. They have many times fired at this town, but they are now afraid of the big guns the white people have here (which they fire at them, because one white man was killed by Kosoko's agents), and so they attack the people travelling on the Abbeokuta road. Twice they have fired at parties and kidnapped several persons. The King of Porto Novo is our enemy, and as Kosoko's friend joins him to make war upon this town. I therefore have sent some of my forces to chastise him, and thus compel him to make friendship and open the road that the merchants here may get palm-oil, and if you could only grant our desire to destroy Lagos, secure that wicked man Kosoko, and bring back Akitoye to Lagos, then we fear not, the whole country will enjoy peace, and if the Slave Trade is put down at Lagos there will not be much more war in the country.

But the particular word I mention to you this morning is, that I and all the chiefs and people of Abbeokuta are most anxious to make friendship with you and all the English. We bow before your Queen and Government, and pray you to make a treaty with us. We promise to keep the law you give us by your help, for if we have English trade we do not want Slave Trade. Hoping our petition will be granted and wishing you peace.

OBBA SHORON

Viscount Palmerston to the Lords Commissioners of the Admiralty
Foreign Office, September 27, 1851

My Lords,
I have to inform you that Her Majesty's Government have given their attentive consideration to the state of the Slave Trade on the western coast of Africa, and have observed with great satisfaction the success which has attended the exertions of Her Majesty's squadron on that station in putting down that piratical practice.

The watchful activity of Her Majesty's cruizers, the multiplication of treaties with the native chiefs, and the operations last year at the Gallinas, appear to have nearly rooted out the Slave Trade from the coast north of the Line.

There remain, however, two persevering offenders, the King of Dahomey and the Chief of Lagos, who still refuse to yield to persuasion, and who continue to thwart and to frustrate the measures of Her Majesty's Government. But Her Majesty's Government cannot any longer permit that the accomplishment of a great purpose, which has been steadily pursued by the British Government and nation for more than a quarter of a century by immense exertions and with great sacrifices, shall be marred and defeated by the criminal and piratical resistance of two barbarous African chiefs.

Her Majesty's Government have twice sent a mission to the King of Dahomey to endeavour to induce him to give up Slave Trade, and on both occasions an offer was made to him of compensation in money for a limited time for any pecuniary loss which he might sustain by foregoing the presents which he has been in the habit of receiving from the slave-traders.

To these overtures and offers of Her Majesty's Government, the King of Dahomey turned a deaf ear, and no sooner were the British missions gone, than he recommenced his usual preparations for his periodical slave-hunts. Her Majesty's officers had endeavoured to persuade him to desist from the barbarous practice of murdering prisoners on public festivals, and the only result was the murder of ten or eleven victims in the very presence of Her Majesty's officers.

The town of Abbeokuta, on the River Ogu, about 60 miles inland from Lagos, and about 150 miles from Abomey, has been the scene of successful exertions by British missionaries, who have drawn thither many emancipated negroes from Sierra Leone, and have instructed many of the natives in the doctrines of Christianity.

Her Majesty's Government necessarily take an interest in the welfare of a town which seems destined to be a centre from which the lights of Christianity and civilization may be spread over the adjoining countries. Her Majesty's officers sent to Abomey heard that the King of Dahomey intended to direct one of his slave-hunts against Abbeokuta, and they urgently in the name of the British Government requested him to abstain from such an attack.

The officer commanding Her Majesty's Naval Force on the west coast of Africa followed up this intercession by a stronger representation, and informed the Dahomey Chief, by a letter, that if he attacked Abbeokuta, his port of Whydah would be blockaded.

But the Dahomey Chief, deaf to entreaties, regardless of warnings, and confident in his own strength, marched, nevertheless, last spring against Abbeokuta with a large force, and if the people of the place had not been assisted by European skill in planning their defence, and by arms and ammunition, to repel the attack, this interesting community would no doubt have shared the fate of the many tribes who have fallen victims to the savage cruelty of the Dahomians. It appears, moreover, from the statements made by the Dahomian prisoners captured on the defeat of the Dahomian army, that no orders had been given to respect, in case of success, either the white inhabitants, the missionaries, or the emancipated negroes; and if Abbeokuta had been taken, all these persons would probably have been reduced to Slavery, or have perished by the sword.

It would not be consistent with the honour and dignity of the British Government, that a warning deliberately given by a British Commodore, in entire conformity with the policy of Her Majesty's Government, and as deliberately set at nought, should be thus disregarded with impunity; and I have to signify to your Lordships the Queen's commands that the Dahomian port of Whydah and the rest of the Dahomian coast should be strictly blockaded.

It is, moreover, Her Majesty's pleasure that the blockade of that port and coast should not be raised until the Chief of Dahomey shall have concluded and signed an agreement, by which he shall bind himself to give up totally and entirely the Slave Trade, to prevent his subjects from practising that crime, and to expel all foreign slave-traders from his territory; to abandon the practice of human sacrifices; and to protect all missionaries who may come to reside within the range of his authority.

Of course no money-compensation can now be given him for any pecuniary loss which he may incur by abandoning Slave Trade. As the principal revenue of this chief is derived from the commerce which passes through Whydah, there seems good reason to expect that such a blockade will be effectual for its purpose.

The Chief of Lagos appears by all accounts to be a barbarous savage who has been put up and is supported by a set of slave-traders who have established themselves on the Island of Lagos; and it appears that his authority, which is scarcely more than nominal, is nearly confined to the island and town of Lagos.

It seems that this chief, and the slave-traders of whom he is the mouth-piece, greatly encouraged the King of Dahomey to make his recent attack upon Abbeokuta, under a notion that there is a connection between the establishment of the missionaries and the suppression of the Slave Trade; and that by destroying the missionaries, they would impede the suppression of Slave Trade.

Her Majesty's Government have been informed by Captain Denham, by Mr Crowther, a missionary who has been at Abbeokuta and at Lagos, and by Mr Beecroft, Her Majesty's Consul for the Bights of Benin and Biafra, that there would be no great difficulty in sending into Lagos the small force which would be sufficient for the purpose of expelling the present chief and the slave-traders by whom he is supported, and for re-establishing in his stead the former chief, Akitoye, who was expelled by the slave-traders on account of his intention to enter into a treaty for the suppression of the Slave Trade.

It is the Queen's pleasure that the Commodore on the west coast of Africa should be instructed to consider the practicability of such an operation, and to undertake it if it could be accomplished without much difficulty or risk.

The most desirable result would be, the expulsion of the present chief, and the restoration of Akitoye, with whom an engagement could be made for putting an end to Slave Trade, and for not permitting slave-traders to reside at Lagos; and any such engagement made by Akitoye would be faithfully carried into execution.

Any engagement to that effect made by the present chief would probably be observed only so long as he was strictly watched and forcibly prevented from breaking it.

If Lagos, instead of being a nest for slave-traders were to become a port for lawful trade, it would, in connection with the navigable river which there discharges itself into the sea, become an important outlet for the commerce of a large range of country in the interior, and instead of being a den of barbarism, would be a diffusing centre of civilization.

PALMERSTON

OCTOBER 1851

Consul Beecroft to Viscount Palmerston (received December 9)
Clarence, Fernando Po, October 4, 1851

My Lord,

I have the honour to communicate that on the 21st ultimo, Mr Vice-Consul Fraser arrived here from Whydah in Her Majesty's brig "Harlequin", Commander Wilmot. He stated that he had a desire to see me personally. On his landing at Whydah, a letter was handed to him by Mr Prior, agent for Messrs Hutton, from Guezo, King of Dahomey, stating at the same time that a deputation from Abomey arrived at the Fort, and requested him to write the King's mouth to Her Majesty the Queen of England. He wrote the accompanying letter through Madaki, the interpreter. Mr Vice-Consul Fraser acceded to Guezo's request, and proceeded to Abomey. Whilst there he received a letter from Obba Shoron, second in command of the Abbeokutian army at Badagry, with 1,000 men for the protection of the Badagrians against the Lagos people. A copy of Mr Vice-Consul Fraser's reply to Obba Shoron I herewith enclose with a copy of Guezo's letter to Her Majesty the Queen of England. The "Harlequin" sailed on the 24th for Whydah.

On Mr Vice-Consul Fraser's safe arrival at his post, he will forward to me a full detail of his mission to Abomey. He stated that Guezo was anxious for presents, such as muskets, bayonets, powder, shot, and shell, to annihilate the Abbeokutians, if possible. At present I have declined to accede to Guezo's request, as the soldier with a big head has already paid him the visit he requested, and found whatever he had to state relative to signing treaties was all twaddle. He never intends it until Her Majesty's Government deem it fit to coerce him to the path. His letter is what I have already stated; he is determined not to come to the point for the best of all reasons. I do declare he is not the despot generally reported; he has not his own will.

I shall wait your Lordship's directions ere I proceed for Whydah, to accede to Guezo's request.

JOHN BEECROFT

Enclosure 1
Vice-Consul Fraser to Obba Shoron, second in command at Abbeokuta

Whydah, September 9, 1851

Sir,

Your letter, dated Badagry, at the beginning of August, reached me at Abomey, through the King of Dahomey's hands, who told me it came through the Anagoo Country. He knew well where it was from. It has since been stolen from me, and I have left the King's place in consequence.

I could not obtain an answer from the King respecting his movements and motives towards Kosoko, but I suspect he will assist him.

Abbeokuta is marked out for a second attack; therefore be vigilant, let no time be lost, nothing left undone, and success is certain.

More care must be taken with official letters in future, as I am now in an unpleasant position through the miscarriage of yours.

Louis Fraser
HBM's Vice-Consul in Dahomey

P.S. I shall be in Abbeokuta as soon as circumstances permit.

Enclosure 2

The King of Dahomey to Her Majesty Queen Victoria
September 7, 1851

The King of Dahomey gives his best compliments to the Queen of England, and thanks her very much for sending me to his country; he has seen me and likes me too much. The same way he send he like, and same way the King of Dahomey will send messenger to Queen of England, by-and-by.

The King says that the palaver that the Queen of England send him about no block Abbeokuta, he hear the King of Abbeokuta (Foolaka*) was the King's friend before; that Foolaka send him children to the King of Dahomey, and say Go block one country for him (called Keada), and the King block that country for him. If Foolaka live, he, the King of Dahomey, block Keada; and if he dies, he can block for him; because the King of Dahomey block Keada for Foolaka. The Abbeokutians go block two countries for Dahomey, King side (one is called Ba-gee and the

*Is now dead.

other To-soo); the Abbeokuta people catch all the Cabooceers, for those countries, and cut the head for all. The above is the reason the King of Dahomey get vexed with Abbeokuta, and as he passed, he give 20,000 men for one of these countries, and also leaving some men in each of the other countries as he passed; is the reason he no block Abbeokuta properly. The reason he block Abbeokuta again is, that last time the Abbeokuta people catch and kill plenty of his men and also his wives, and keep them to make their own wives.

The King says myself have live this country, by-and-by me and him can settle the slave palaver.

Mayo X (his mark)

P.S. The King say, anything belonging to the Queen of England live at Abbeokuta; he can see everyone in his own hand.

The King say this black man kill this white man (Gee, at Badagry); if the Queen of England send to him, he can block his place; he no like black man for kill white man for any way.

Mr Addington to the Secretary of the Admiralty
Foreign Office, October 8, 1851

Sir,

I have laid before Viscount Palmerston Commodore Bruce's despatch of the 3rd of July last, together with its original enclosures on the subject of a mission which was about to be undertaken by Commander Wilmot, of Her Majesty's steamer "Harlequin", and Mr Beecroft, Her Majesty's Consul in the Bights of Benin and Biafra, for the purpose of endeavouring to induce the King of Dahomey to sign the Treaty for the suppression of the Slave Trade from his dominions, which had upon a former occasion been proposed to him by Mr Beecroft and Lieutenant Forbes, of Her Majesty's ship "Bonetta", without success, but which Commodore Bruce thinks it is not improbable he may now agree to conclude, in consequence of his subsequent severe defeat by the Yoruba nation in his attack upon Abbeokuta.

I have also laid before Viscount Palmerston a further despatch of the 31st of July last from Commodore Bruce, together with its original enclosures, on the subject of an attack which had recently been made on Badagry by the people of Lagos.

I am directed by Lord Palmerston to request in reply, that you will state to the Lords Commissioners of the Admiralty, that his Lordship is of opinion that the instructions mentioned in his letter to their Lordships of the 27th ultimo, about the King of Dahomey, and about Whydah and Lagos, should be sent to Commodore Bruce; but that he should be told that if, when he receives those instructions, a satisfactory arrangement shall have been made either with the King of Dahomey, or with the Chief of Lagos, or with both, so much of those instructions as relates to the Chief with whom the satisfactory arrangment shall have been made, or the whole instruction, if a satisfactory arrangement shall have been made with both, shall be considered as cancelled. But if either or both of those chiefs shall have rejected the proposals made to them for the complete abandonment and entire suppression of the Slave Trade within the limits of their authority, then those instructions should be considered as in force, and should be acted upon in regard to either, or to both of those chiefs, as the case may be.

The draft of Treaty which was to be proposed to the King of Dahomey in 1849 was more advantageous to him than the conditions which Her Majesty's Government would now be willing to offer him; and King Guezo of Dahomey must have been prepared for a curtailment of those conditions by the last letter which Lord Palmerston wrote to him, dated the 11th of October, 1850. If, however, he shall have accepted the Draft of Treaty drawn up in 1849, it will of course be ratified; but if he shall have rejected it, then and in such case the fuller arrangements and the less advantageous conditions stated in the instructions contained in Lord Palmerston's letter to the Lords of the Admiralty above referred to, should be exacted from him.

Pecuniary compensation may properly be offered in return for a voluntary engagement, but pecuniary compensation need not be given for an engagement extorted by force; moreover, at the time when the draft of Convention of 1849 was prepared, Her Majesty's Government had been led to believe that King Guezo had abandoned or was about to abandon the barbarous practice of human sacrifices; but what passed during the mission of Mr Beecroft and Lieutenant F. E. Forbes to Abomey proved that this practice is still continued, and that there was no intention of giving it up; a stipulation upon that subject ought, therefore, to be imposed upon King Guezo.

H.U. ADDINGTON

The Lords Commissioners of the Admiralty to
Commodore Bruce

Viscount Palmerston, Her Majesty's Principal Secretary of State for Foreign Affairs, having signified to us the Queen's pleasure that instructions should be given to you to take proceedings against the King of Dahomey and Chief of Lagos, we send you herewith a copy of Lord Palmerston's letter, dated the 27th September last; and we require and direct you to carry out the intentions of Her Majesty's

Government as therein expressed, except as hereinafter modified.

We send you, at the time, a copy of a letter from the Under-Secretary of State for Foreign Affairs, dated the 8th instant, by which you are to be guided in carrying out the foregoing instructions, or in abstaining from doing so, according to the pending proceedings; and you will be strictly guided by the views of Viscount Palmerston, as therein pointed out.

With respect to that part of the instructions respecting Lagos, we leave the mode of carrying it out to your discretion and judgement.

Should you consider a small steam-vessel of use in any operations you may have to undertake in pursuance of these orders, and you are able to obtain such a vessel, you have our authority to hire it for the purpose.

And finally, we direct you not to keep possession of Lagos, nor to remain there beyond what is absolutely necessary.

Given under our hands, this 14th day of October, 1851.

F. T. BARING
R.D. DUNDAS

By command of their Lordships,

W.A.B. HAMILTON

NOVEMBER 1851

Commodore Bruce to the Secretary of the Admiralty
"Penelope", Island of St Thomas, November 1, 1851

Sir,

In my despatch dated the 31st July, 1851, I had the honour to acquaint you, for the information of the Lords Commissioners of the Admiralty, that I had written letters to the King of Lagos and the Chief of Porto Novo, warning them against molesting British subjects at Badagry. The former has returned my letter without any written comment, but sent a verbal message to the effect that he wanted no communication with the English.

It is necessary you should acquaint their Lordships that the natural-born British subjects at Badagry consist of a few merchants and missionaries, who have clearly a right to the protection which would be afforded them in any other part of the world; besides these, there are several hundreds of liberated Africans, who, if they have not a legal, have certainly a moral claim on our support; their freedom has been solemnly pronounced by competent British tribunals; many of them have embraced the doctrines and practices of Christianity. In the centre of a slave-trading people they have withstood the temptation of the great pecuniary gains to be had from bartering their fellow-men, and have devoted their energies to the exercise of legitimate occupations. Their interference in the war now pending between the Chief of Lagos and the natives of Badagry and Abbeokuta has been compulsory; they have been obliged to fight, not that Akitoye might resume the throne from which he has been expelled, but from the certainty that if the reigning Chief, Kosoko, conquers their adopted country, they will inevitably be doomed to Slavery for the remainder of their lives.

Agreeably with their Lordships' directions signified to me in your letter of the 2nd September, 1851, I have communicated with the Governor of Sierra Leone, and given instructions to the senior officers of the North and Bights Divisions of the station, respecting the conveyance of arms, ammunition, and men, for the service of the Abbeokutians; the assistance thus to be afforded will, I have no doubt, be of the utmost benefit in bringing the war to a favourable conclusion; but I trust that the King of Lagos having obstinately declined any intercourse with Her Majesty's officers, and having insultingly returned my letter, although the purport of it was merely to request him not to allow the persons or property of British subjects to be injured by the people under his control, coupled with the fact of his having forcibly detained an Englishman on shore for four days, while he was shipping a cargo of slaves, will induce their Lordships to authorize me to adopt more stringent measures against him. I believe that every nation has a right to communicate with another in any matter that may affect the interests of its subjects; and that the refusal of the King of Lagos to receive the friendly warnings of Her Majesty's officers is tantamount to a declaration that these warnings will not be attended to.

The legitimate trade of Lagos is considerable; it is, moreover, the principal slave-mart remaining in Western Africa. I am of opinion that the establishment of a commercial blockade of the coast would not only bring its turbulent chief to a proper sense of his duty with regard to foreign powers, but would be the means of completely suppressing the Slave Trade in his territory, and afford a salutary lesson to the neighbouring native Kings.

If their Lordships think proper to authorize me to establish such a blockade, I request that I may be permitted to extend it to Porto Novo and Whydah (the sea-port of Dahomey), if the course of events should render it expedient to do so.

I enclose for their Lordships' inspection, my letter, as it was returned by the Chief of Lagos.

H.W. BRUCE

Enclosure

Commodore Bruce to Kosoko, the Chief of Lagos

Captain Jones has transmitted to me a copy of the note which he sent to you on the 25th of June relative to the war between Lagos and Badagry. I entirely approve of the caution he has given you, and as I shall remain in the neighbourhood, I have desired him to acquaint me with any case that may come to his knowledge, where British subjects have been injured by persons under your control. The English residents in these countries are here to advance the moral and social condition of the natives, they take no part in their quarrels, and therefore should never be molested; if they should suffer in person or property in consequence of your war with Badagry, it will be my duty to inflict condign punishment on the offending parties.

Given under my hand, on board Her Britannic Majesty's ship "Penelope", at Prince's, the 29th day of July, 1851.

H.W. BRUCE

Commodore Bruce to the Secretary of the Admiralty
"Penelope", Isle of St Thomas, November 1, 1851

Sir,

In my despatch of the 27th ultimo I acquainted you that Commander F. E. Forbes had gone to Badagry in the "Sampson", ★ I have now the honour to request you will inform the Lords Commissioners of the Admiralty, that Mr Consul Beecroft, whom I have seen at Fernando Po, will also proceed this day to Badagry and Abbeokuta, on a similar mission to that which Commander Forbes is employed upon.

Mr Beecroft is satisfied that Abbeokuta is safe from an attack by the Dahomians for some weeks to come, as the rivers which must be passed will not be fordable before February or March. Supplies of ammunition and arms, if not of men, will have been forwarded to Obba Shoron, in the meantime.

Mr Beecroft will also go up the Benin River with the view of ascertaining its capacity for facilitating the destruction of Lagos, should such a proceeding become necessary. He is of opinion that to give an effectual blow to the Slave Traffic in that quarter, Lagos ought to be taken under the

★Editor's note: in the original papers, this despatch does not appear to have been included.

protection of England, but he is at the same time aware of the pestilential nature of its climate and position. On this subject I would remind their Lordships that the European trade with Lagos is very considerable, particularly in Hamburgh vessels; and, moreover, that the second paragraph of Article VI of the Convention between Her Majesty and the King of the French, signed at London, May 29, 1845, stipulates that no part of the coast of Africa shall be occupied without the consent of the two High Contracting Parties. Akitoye does not appear to me to be a man likely to maintain his place by physical influence, if he could be reinstated in his seat of Government. I intend to be at Badagry and Lagos in the course of December.

H.W. Bruce

Consul Beecroft to Viscount Palmerston
(received January 7, 1852)
"Bloodhound", off Lagos, November 26, 1851

My Lord,
I have the honour to communicate, for the information of your Lordship, that I embarked on board of Her Majesty's steamer "Bloodhound" on the 10th instant, accompanied by King Akitoye and his suite, and arrived off Lagos on the 13th. Communicated with Commander Wilmot of Her Majesty's sloop "Harlequin", who informed me that he had discovered a safe boat-channel into the River Ogu; and he had visited Kosoko, the present Chief of Lagos, and was kindly received. That it was his impression that he would accede to my terms, if proposed. It appeared to me a favourable opportunity to enter into a negotiation with the said chief at once.

The same evening Her Majesty's brig "Waterwitch", Commander Gardner, arrived to relieve Her Majesty's sloop "Harlequin".

After a short conference I decided upon entering into a negotiation in compliance with your Lordship's despatches received 30th of June, 1851, dated October 11, 1850 and February 20 and 21, 1851.

It was arranged, in conjunction with Commanders Wilmot, Gardner, and Lieutenant-Commander Russell Patey, as there were on board Her Majesty's steamer "Bloodhound" 200 muskets for the protection of Abbeokuta, that I should proceed immediately for Badagry, land the muskets, and deliver Commander Wilmot's letter to Commander Coote, Her Majesty's steamer "Volcano", ordering him to proceed to Lagos, so as to enable him to form a respectable escort under a flag of truce to the present Chief of Lagos, to whom I addressed a letter, and left it with Commander Wilmot to forward.

November 14. Her Majesty's steamer "Bloodhound" weighed at 11 o'clock, and anchored off Badagry at 4 o'clock. Fired a gun and hoisted a signal for a canoe. Did not succeed in getting one until next morning.

November 15, Saturday. I landed at 10 o'clock, accompanied by Lieutenant-Commander Patey and King Akitoye. He was received with demonstrations of unbounded joy. Shortly after I held a short conference with him and his chiefs relative to Lagos and his accompanying me. It was arranged that he should accompany me. The flints and muskets could not be completed landing until Monday. Embarked again on Tuesday the 18th at 3.30 PM and anchored off Lagos at 8.30 PM. No "Volcano". Commanders Wilmot and Gardner came on board. It was arranged to start from Her Majesty's sloop "Harlequin" at 9 o'clock, with ten boats, to proceed at once to the town of Lagos.

November 19. Daylight, strong symptoms of a tornado; showed itself 9.30; it came down in torrents of rain. It continued so long that our visit to Kosoko was deferred until next day.

November 20. Daylight, fine dry weather. Left Her Majesty's sloop "Harlequin" at 6.30, with ten boats and flag of truce. Landed on a sandy point at the eastern entrance of the river, to wait for the water to rise to enable the heavy boats to enter. There are here a few huts, and two stores or sheds belonging to Senhor Marcos and Senhor Nobre, Brazilians.

A messenger arrived from Kosoko, stating that if we proceeded to Lagos with ten boats, we should be fired upon; it was his wish that one boat only should go. I remonstrated with Senhor Marcos on the entire absurdity of Kosoko preventing a proper escort to accompany Her Majesty's Representatives on a mission of peace and amity; that it was a national form of all the nations in the world. Senhor Marcos said that he had remonstrated with the chief to no avail; he would not listen to any other sentiment but what he first stated. I was on the point of returning, but after mature deliberation I told the messenger, through my interpreter, that one boat was not sufficient to take all the officers intended for the conference; I would come with two boats, well knowing, at the same time, that we were going to be placed in imminent danger, with such a blood-thirsty chief as Kosoko. We had to wait until the messenger returned, which was an hour, with the chief's permission. There were on this point of sand one hundred armed men, sent to watch our movements, no doubt. Senhores Marcos and Nobre, I must state, were very attentive.

10 o'clock, we started in the "Harlequin" and "Waterwitch's" gigs; Senhor Marcos accompanied me, and Commander Wilmot, Commander Gardner, Lieutenant-Commander Patey, and my interpreter, in the second gig. We arrived at the town in one hour and twenty minutes. We were ushered into Senhor Marcos' house, there kept in

suspense for two hours before we were ushered into the presence of the Chief, Kosoko. He was surrounded with armed men, with a host of retainers on each side of the court-yard.

I opened the conference by saluting him, stating that I was much pleased at having an opportunity given me as the Queen of England's Representative, of communicating to him, the purport of my mission.

Firstly, was the chief desirous to become friends with England, and sign a Treaty for the total suppression of the Slave Trade within the limits of his territories? He replied that he was not his own master, but under the King of Benin. I told the chief that I was going to Benin, and would inter-cede with him also to sign the above-mentioned treaty.

I had previously asked the chief, supposing the King of Benin, his master, signed the Treaty, if he was prepared to do the same; he distinctly stated, through his Prime Minister, Tapaa, that he would not enter into any treaty with the English, and did not wish their friendship. I again put the same question as above, if he, Kosoko, was ready and will-ing to sign the Treaty with his master, the King of Benin, as he had already acknowledged him to be so?

The chief then stated that he had not up to the present received any power or authority from the King of Benin to rule as King of Lagos. He repeated the same as above, that the King might sign, but he, Kosoko would not, nor had he any desire to do so. It is quite certain that the King of Benin will not give him that power, so long as he is certain Akitoye is alive, for he has the emblems of authority from the late and present King of Benin, who was crowned at the city of Benin when I was in that river last March. Of the further details of this conference, my Lord, I send a copy.

Finding, after our conference, that our terms were rejected, it was decided to collect such a show of force as the moment could supply, with the firm belief that such force, judging from the character of African chiefs, would have the effect, by simple demonstration of our power, to cause him to accede to our terms. We entered the river with a flag of truce, and but three guns were fired by the "Bloodhound" on entering the river, at what was considered outposts firing without authority. The flags of truce were flying until off the town, when the fire from the shore became so galling as to render the flag of truce nugatory. On being hauled down by us, a general fire in return was opened from us by the boats and Her Majesty's steamer "Bloodhound". The latter's assistance as a cover for the boats was unfortunately lost by her grounding at high-water, within range of the town, but not sufficiently so to afford that support to the boats that was so necessary. The waters were cleared of canoes, and a considerable part of the town burnt; but the mud-walls and very narrow streets afforded so great an advantage to the enemy, who were swarming in vast numbers, and proved themselves such good marksmen, that it was thought advisable to recall the people to their boats, as our people suffered much.

The "Bloodhound" remained on shore until high-water, when she was hove-off into $2\frac{1}{2}$ fathoms, and remained for the night.

The senior officer and a part of the boats left the river for their ships. The following morning early, the expedition was withdrawn, the senior officer being fearful of fever.

JOHN BEECROFT

Enclosure
Consul Beecroft to Commander T. G. Forbes
"Bloodhound", at sea, off Elmina Chica, November 22, 1851
Sir,
Having had an interview with the usurper chief, Kosoko, and used every available means directed in my instructions

from Lord Palmerston, to make a treaty with him for the suppression of the foreign Slave Trade, the only answer that I could obtain was, that he did not wish to be friends with the English. I have no alternative but to apply to you (as senior officer in the Bights) for a sufficient force to compel him to make a treaty, or dethrone him and replace the rightful heir, Akitoye.

You will see in the despatches received by me from Her Majesty's Government, that it is their earnest wish that decided and peremptory measures should be taken, and if necessary by force of arms.

I call your attention to the necessity of acting promptly, before the war breaks out, which may be expected daily.

My opinion is, that prompt and immediate measures ought to be taken, the water being favourable across the Bar at this time, which if delayed would in all probability prevent any coercive measures until next year.

I request you will take into consideration my views on this subject to enable me to carry out the wishes of the Government.

JOHN BEECROFT

DECEMBER 1851

Commodore Bruce to the Secretary of the Admiralty
"Penelope", Sierra Leone, December 6, 1851

Sir,

I request you will be pleased to acquaint the Lords Commissioners of the Admiralty, that their order dated 14th October last, directing me to carry out the instructions of Her Majesty's Government relative to the King of Dahomey and the Chief of Lagos, having reached me at Ascension on the 20th ultimo, I sailed immediately for this place to concert measures with the Governor for obtaining a supply of arms and ammunition for the people of Badagry, and to receive on board as many of the liberated Africans as might volunteer to join the cause of the Abbeokutians.

After consulting his Excellency I obtained from the ordnance storekeeper, for conveyance to Badagry:

2 light field-pieces (3-pounders) with 300 rounds of powder and shot.

159 muskets, flint-lock, with bayonets.

28,000 musket-ball cartridges and 2 barrels of flints.

The Africans would not volunteer without a promise of being paid for their services; under this circumstance I declined to receive them.

My despatches will have apprised their Lordships of the failure which has attended my endeavours to treat on favourable terms with the King of Dahomey and the Chief of Lagos. I am of opinion that the course about to be pursued will bring about the object in view, and compel these barbarous rulers to put a stop to Slave Trade in their dominions.

I cannot tell the exact limits of the coast subject to the authority of the Chiefs of Dahomey and Lagos, but the Foreign Office chart which was supplied to me on leaving England, and the reports I have received from Captain Jones, the senior naval officer in the Bights, and the several officers serving there, prove that Slave Trade exists (except at Badagry) from longitude 1° to 4°30′ east; I shall therefore blockade the whole of that line of territory.

I send you herewith a notification of the blockade and a copy of my order on the subject to the officers commanding Her Majesty's ships on this station, which I trust their Lordships will approve of.

In the absence of any report from Mr Beecroft, relative to the result of the mission to Dahomey, I should have delayed issuing the notification of blockade until my arrival in the Bights, but Mr Fraser's communication [to Obba Shoron, on 9th September, 1851] held out so little prospect of matters being amicably settled, that to prevent unnecessary inconvenience to several merchant-vessels about to sail for that quarter, I deemed it but proper and just that they should be apprised forthwith of the steps about to be taken. I have also given due notice of the blockade to the several British and foreign functionaries on the Coast, and to Rear-Admiral Henderson in the Brazils.

I believe there is sometimes as much as six feet water on the bar of the Lagos River; a small steam-vessel, therefore, would be of infinite service, but I am sorry to say I cannot hire one at Sierra Leone.

It is my intention to proceed towards the Bights tomorrow, and I have made arrangements for meeting Mr Consul Beecroft, Commander Forbes, and Akitoye, late Chief of Lagos, in the neighbourhood of Badagry.

H.W. BRUCE

Enclosure 1
Notification of blockade
"Penelope", Sierra Leone, December 6, 1851

In compliance with instructions from Her Majesty's Government, it is hereby notified that a blockade of all ports and places (except Badagry) situated in the Bight of Benin, from longitude 1° to 4° 30′ east of Greenwich, will forthwith be established by me with an efficient force; and no merchant-vessel will be permitted to hold any communication whatever with the ports and places interdicted, from and after the 1st day of January next.

H.W. BRUCE, *Commodore and Commander-in-Chief of Her Britannic Majesty's Naval Forces on the West Coast of Africa*

Enclosure 2
Order issued by Commodore Bruce
"Penelope", Sierra Leone, December 6, 1851

General Memo

The respective captains, commanders, and officers commanding Her Majesty's ships and vessels on the west coast of Africa will receive herewith a notification of my intention to establish a complete blockade of all the ports and places in the Bights of Benin (except Badagry), from longitude 1° to 4° 30´ east of Greenwich, and they are to supply a copy of the same to the masters of all merchant-vessels they may happen to fall in with, inserting in the log-books of such vessels the fact of their having done so.

The duties devolving on the commanders and officers of the ships of the blockading squadron are of a most delicate nature: while, on the one hand, they are required to carry out the blockade in a strict and impartial manner, they are, on the other hand, enjoined not to give occasion to foreign Governments to complain of any undue severity or annoyance in the accomplishment of this service.

Vessels of war are not to be interfered with in any way, and merchant-vessels are not to be detained unless they are found breaking the blockade after due notice of its existence has been inserted in their log-books, and signed by the boarding officer.

It must be borne in mind that the blockade is intended to bring about the suppression of the Traffic in Slaves; therefore it should be the endeavour of Her Majesty's officers, in the accomplishment of this object, to occasion as little inconvenience as possible to lawful traders.

Boats sent away to board, or on detached service, are to have an ensign and pendant flying; the officer in charge is to be of commissioned rank, to wear his proper uniform, and to be particularly instructed not to search any vessel belonging to a nation that has not conceded that right to Great Britain.

Commanding officers are required to receive on board their respective ships, British and foreign residents, and others, who may be desirous of leaving any of the blockaded ports or places for protection, or to wait an opportunity of being transferred to merchant-vessels.

No person belonging to the squadron is to be permitted to land on any part of the blockaded coast, without the permission of the Senior Officer present.

H.W. Bruce, *Commodore*

Commander Heath to the Secretary of the Admiralty
"Niger", Sierra Leone, December 17, 1851

Sir,

I have the honour to inform you that on the 27th November, 1851, I left Lagos under orders from the Senior Officer of the Bights, Commander T.G. Forbes, of the "Philomel", to carry his and Mr Beecroft's (the Consul) despatches to the Commodore. I first proceeded to Ascension, and thence to Sierra Leone, where I arrived on the 17th.

I find the homeward-bound mail-steamer on the point of starting for England, and as I have not yet fallen in with the Commodore, and there is no letter addressed to the Secretary of the Admiralty amongst the despatches with which I am charged, I think it my duty, in accordance with Article 56, chapter 5 of the Admiralty's instructions, to request you will submit to their Lordships the following account of events which have recently occurred at Lagos.

About the middle of November, Her Majesty's steamer "Bloodhound" arrived at Lagos from Fernando Po with the Consul, Mr Beecroft, on board. Mr Beecroft immediately put himself into communication with Commander Wilmot, of Her Majesty's steamer "Harlequin" (the cruiser stationed off Lagos), and proceeded with the boats of that vessel and the "Waterwitch" to ascend the river with the intention of endeavouring to make a treaty with the King of Lagos.

In crossing the Bar the boats were met by messengers from Kosoko, the King, begging them not to come up in force, as the inhabitants of the town were much excited, and he could not answer for the consequences, should they do so. Accordingly, the armed boats remained at the river's mouth, whilst Mr Beecroft, Commanders Wilmot and Gardner, and Lieutenant Patey, went up to the King's Palace in two gigs. They were received with much honour and ceremony, but the King refused to make any treaty whatever with Her Majesty Queen Victoria.

Mr Beecroft then proceeded round the Bights in search of the Senior Officer, Commander T.G. Forbes, of Her Majesty's brig "Philomel", and made a requisition, in virtue of which the whole force was assembled off Lagos by the evening of the 23rd November.

On the 24th, Commander Forbes called together the Commanders of the vessels to consult with Mr Beecroft on the steps to be pursued. Mr Beecroft produced three documents. No. 1 was an extract from a letter of Lord Palmerston's to the Board of Admiralty, detailing the political state of Lagos, and suggesting that with a view to the suppression of the Slave Trade, it might be advisable to dethrone Kosoko, the present King of Lagos, and set up his rival, Akitoye. No. 2 was a despatch from Lord Palmerston to Mr Beecroft, relative to the support to be given to Abbeokuta. No. 3 was from Lord Palmerston to Mr Beecroft, instructing him to endeavour to make an anti-slave-trading treaty with Kosoko; failing in that he was to call upon the naval officers to give him such a force as would ensure his personal safety, and he was to obtain another interview with Kosoko, and point out to him the strength of England; the relative weakness of Lagos on account of its proximity to the sea; and the fact that there was a rival claimant to his throne; and in short, Mr Beecroft was to use the strongest possible arguments to induce Kosoko to make a treaty.

After due deliberation, it was resolved that No.1, being merely a letter from Lord Palmerston to the Board of

Admiralty, could not be considered in the light of instructions to Mr Beecroft. No. 2 was important, because it was well known that the meditated attack by the King of Dahomey on the town of Abbeokuta might perhaps be averted by British interference at Lagos. No. 3 appeared exactly to meet existing circumstances. The case which had arisen was foreseen by Lord Palmerston, and specifically provided for. Mr Beecroft had failed in obtaining a treaty; the next step was for him to go up and use stronger arguments with the King, and for us to support him with an armed force.

A channel across the Bar fit for the "Bloodhound" had been surveyed and buoyed by Mr Earle, master of the "Harlequin", assisted by Mr Harris, of the "Waterwitch", and at daylight on the 25th, the "Bloodhound", with the boats and all the marines, crossed the Bar in safety. The "Bloodhound" carried a flag of truce; and, in addition to this, Mr Beecroft accompanied Commander Wilmot in his gig, advanced fully 200 yards ahead of the flotilla, with another large and most conspicuous white flag. On crossing the Bar, an ineffective but heavy fire of musketry was opened from the Point; but this being four miles distant from the town, it was considered that it might have been done without the sanction of Kosoko, and accordingly no notice was taken of it, and the white flags were kept flying. The steamer grounded when within one mile and half of the town; and after an unsuccessful attempt to get off, the boats formed a line and pulled up the river. A gun from the shore now opened fire on the boats, and as they continued to advance, other large guns and a very heavy and well-sustained, but owing to the distance, harmless fire of musketry, was opened upon them. The flags of truce were then hauled down; and keeping all the boats out of musket-range, the gunboats commenced action with shrapnel shell and round-shot, whilst the "Niger" occasionally sent a shell towards the Point at the river's mouth.

The cannonade having continued for an hour or so, a landing with a view to firing the town was resolved on; the boats accordingly pulled in simultaneously for one spot, and about 160 or 180 men were landed, the remainder guarding the boats and protecting the subsequent embarkation. The natives made a most determined resistance, and a most skilful use of the advantages of their position. The town, or at least that part of it in which we landed, consists of narrow streets, intersecting one another in every direction. We were thus exposed to a flanking fire down every street which debouched on our line of advance; and the natives, when driven from one post ran by backways to take up a new position further on. After advancing some 200 or 300 yards, finding the resistance by no means diminishing, but, on the contrary, that the number of our opponents was increasing at every turning; and having already suffered a loss of two officers killed and six or seven men wounded, it was determined that to continue the advance would be imprudent, and we therefore fired all the neighbouring houses, and returned to the boats, and thence to the "Bloodhound". The fire continued to burn with great fury for four hours, and there were two large explosions, but there was no wind all the day; and I am inclined to think the houses destroyed formed but a small portion of the whole city.

It can be no exaggeration to say that there were 5,000 men in arms against us. A beach about one mile and a half in length was lined with musketry, and a continuous and most heavy fire was kept up along its whole face. Besides this every house was a small fortification, and there were five or six large guns and many swivels constantly at work.

The "Bloodhound" was got afloat the same night, and the next morning the expedition recrossed the Bar, and on the 27th the ships returned to their cruizing-grounds.

Commander Forbes has, I believe, arranged that in the

event of no submission being made by Kosoko, the "Harlequin" should occasionally annoy him with shells, etc., in order to keep him from attempting any new expedition against the missionary establishment at Badagry. In the meantime he has sent me to Ascension with the wounded, and I am to seek the Commander-in-Chief, and inform him of the state of affairs, and to procure a supply of rockets; and he intends, I believe, to await further instructions.

I am aware that in writing this letter I should merely confine myself to stating the facts for their Lordships' information; but I hope I may be allowed to express a wish that their Lordships will be satisfied that we have done our duty, and that although we had not at the time of my leaving succeeded in bringing Kosoko to his senses, we yet by making good our landing, and firing his town in the face of so determined a resistance, and of such an enormous disparity of force, did as much as was possible under the circumstances to effect.

I enclose a return of the force employed, and of the casualties. It may be considered nearly correct, but not strictly so, except in the case of the "Niger", upon whose ship's company, I am sorry to say, nearly all the loss has fallen. Besides those mentioned in the return, there were many struck more or less with spent-balls.

L.G. HEATH

Enclosure

Return of force employed at the expedition up Lagos River, on the 25th November, 1851

23 boats	2 killed (officers)
5 guns	10 wounded
25 officers	
188 men (seamen)	
53 marines	

Commodore Bruce to the King of Dahomey
"Penelope", Whydah, December 17, 1851

Sir,

In June last you requested that a soldier with a good head might be sent to Abomey to hear something which you wished to be repeated to the Queen, my Sovereign.

Under the impression that you were about to yield to the voice of reason and humanity, and accede to an agreement for the suppression of the infamous Traffic in Slaves, on the terms which were proposed to you by Commander F. E. Forbes and Mr Beecroft in 1850, Mr Fraser, Her Majesty's Vice-Consul at Whydah, complied with your request, and proceeded to Abomey, where, instead of the good result he hoped for, he learnt that your object in seeking the presence of an Englishman at your capital, was to instruct him to convey your application to the Queen for arms and ammunition to enable you to carry on a war against Abbeokuta.

Now you must be aware, because you have been told it repeatedly, that the men of Abbeokuta are looked upon with favour by the British Government, for the reason that they are assisting in the suppression of the Slave Trade; and, therefore, the Queen of England has commanded, not only that no assistance should be given to you, to the prejudice of the Abbeokutians, but in consequence of your former attack on these people, your obstinacy in continuing to sell slaves to the Europeans living in Dahomey who are engaged in that Traffic, and your abominable practice of murdering prisoners on public festivals and other occasions, that your town of Whydah and the coast on the neighbourhood be blockaded, so as to prevent your having any trade, or receiving any supplies whatever from the sea; which blockade is to continue so long as you adhere to your present evil courses.

You have set at nought the many warnings which you have received from the Queen's Government, Commodore Fanshawe, and myself. You are now to be shown that these were not idle words, but meant, in the spirit of friendship, to put you on your guard against listening to the counsel of the slave-traders, who consult their own personal interest, and not your honour and prosperity.

By coming yourself without delay to Whydah, or by sending duly authorized messengers to enter into such a Treaty as I am empowered to make for the total suppression of the Slave Trade, and by preserving peace with Abbeokuta, you may yet save your country and yourself from the ruin and destruction which await it and you.

How can you hope for success in your present course? The Brazilians have given up the Slave Trade, so also have the Spaniards. If you had your barracoons full of slaves you could not sell them to these people, even at one dollar each; properly speaking, you are required not to renew the Slave Trade, for at this moment it may be said to be suppressed.

Dahomey is stated to be rich in various productions useful to the merchants of Europe and America. Let your subjects turn their attention to these, and to the cultivation of the land and its produce, and you will have the support and encouragement of all civilized nations.

The advantageous terms which were formerly offered to you cannot now be given, that is to say, you will not receive any pecuniary compensation from the British Government. If you continue still to hold out, the English will be your enemies, and your brother African Chiefs will be leagued against you to destroy you.

Should you be desirous of retaining your position as King of Dahomey, leave the Abbeokutians to themselves, and prove yourself worthy of the goodwill of the Queen of England.

H. W. BRUCE

Commodore Bruce to the Secretary of the Admiralty
"Penelope", off Lagos, December 19, 1851

Sir,

In accordance with the intimation conveyed in my despatch to you dated December 6, 1851, I sailed from Sierra Leone on the 8th instant. I proceeded along the coast, touched at several places, and arrived here yesterday, when I learned that Commander Thomas Forbes, of the "Philomel", had, on the 25th of November, upon the requisition of Mr Consul Beecroft, entered the River Lagos with an armed force, which resulted in his being led into an engagement with the party under the direction of the Chief, Kosoko.

From the verbal reports I have received, and from information contained in the documents accompanying this despatch, I will endeavour, in as concise a manner as possible, to place the Lords of the Admiralty in possession of the particular circumstances which brought the respective parties into collision.

On the 20th November, Mr Beecroft, accompanied by Commander Wilmot, of the "Harlequin", Commander Gardner, of the "Waterwitch", and Lieutenant Patey, of the "Bloodhound", held a conference with Kosoko and other ruling chiefs at Lagos, and offered them the friendly alliance of Great Britain, on the condition that they relinquished the foreign Slave Trade. On the part of Lagos, these propositions were declined, with the remark that the friendship of England was not wanted.

On the 25th of November, Mr Beecroft having showed Commander Forbes certain instructions from Lord Palmerston, prevailed upon him to send an armed force, with a flag of truce, into the River Lagos. This force was fired at from the town and both banks of the river. The flag of truce was hauled down, a general action commenced, and the men effected a landing, set fire to several houses, returned to their boats, and re-embarked, with the loss of 2 officers killed, and 2 officers and 14 men wounded.

There are circumstances connected with this transaction to which I am reluctantly compelled to draw their Lordships' attention.

In the first place, I regret that Mr Beecroft should have attempted to negotiate with Kosoko, after the failure which attended his endeavours on the 20th November.

Secondly, that in a case where immediate action was not necessary, he should, without consulting me, have requested an officer under my orders to place himself in a position where hostilities were almost inevitable.

Thirdly, because there can be no doubt that the instructions he had received from Lord Palmerston were intended by his Lordship to be carried into execution in conjunction with the Naval Commander-in-Chief at this station.

Fourthly, that a flag of truce should have been displayed under circumstances which could scarcely warrant a hope of its being respected.

Fifthly, that having made an express appointment to meet Mr Beecroft here on the 15th of December, to conduct any operations that might be considered necessary during the present favourable season, which will last until the end of February, the position of affairs now leaves but one course of action open to me, which is, to inflict a summary and retributive punishment upon the chiefs of Lagos.

I am quite certain that Commander Forbes acted from a desire to promote the interests of Her Majesty's service, and I am confident their Lordships will be pleased with the gallantry displayed by him and the officers, seamen, and marines under his command.

I particularly regret the loss which the service has sustained by the death of Mr Dyer and Mr Hall, mates of the

"Niger"; they were both highly meritorious officers, and were killed in the very execution of their duty.

H.W. Bruce

Commodore Bruce to Commander T.G. Forbes
"Penelope", off Lagos, December 19, 1851

Sir,
I have read your reasons for having, on the 24th November, sent an armed force with a flag of truce into the River Lagos.

It appears to me, that after the failure of the negotiation on the 20th of that month, an attempt to treat with the present Chief of Lagos upon any terms, was extremely ill-advised.

While I acknowledge the zeal for the honour of the service which I have no doubt actuated you, I cannot, under all the circumstances of the case, approve of your proceedings.

Hostile operations should, unless on occasions requiring immediate notice, be only commenced under the direction of the Commander-in-Chief. It would have been quite judicious if you had referred Mr Beecroft's application to me or to Captain Jones, particularly as I lost no opportunity of making known in the squadron my intention of being here about this date.

I fully appreciate the gallantry of the parties engaged, and regret the loss which the service has sustained by the death of Mr Dyer and Mr Hall of the "Niger", and the several men who were wounded in the action.

H.W. Bruce

Viscount Palmerston to Consul Beecroft
Foreign Office, December 24, 1851

Sir,

I have received your despatch of the 4th of October, stating that Mr Vice-Consul Fraser has proceeded to Abomey in consequence of an invitation from Guezo, King of Dahomey, and enclosing a translation of a message sent by that chief to the Queen.

I have to state to you that it is not fitting that either you, or Mr Fraser, or any other British officer should under present circumstances go again to Abomey.

The Chief of Dahomey knows what are the desires of the British Government in regard to the Slave Trade; if he is willing to comply with those desires, he can send to Whydah some person duly authorized to conclude an engagement on his part or to signify his readiness to conclude such an engagement with any British officer who may be sent for that purpose to Dahomey; but until such willingness on the part of King Guezo is formally signified, there would be no use in sending any British officer to Abomey.

Instructions to the above effect have been sent to Vice-Consul Fraser, and I have at the same time directed him to address a letter to the Chief of Dahomey, reminding him that the British Government expects and requires that he shall abstain from any attack on Abbeokuta.

PALMERSTON

JANUARY 1852

Commodore Bruce to the Secretary of the Admiralty
"Penelope", off Lagos, January 2, 1852

Sir,

I have the honour to report, for the information of the Lords Commissioners of the Admiralty, that their Lordships' instructions of the 14th October, and the wishes of Her Majesty's Secretary of State for Foreign Affairs, as far as respects Lagos, have been faithfully fulfilled by the expulsion of the slave-dealing Chief, Kosoko, and his people; the utter destruction of his town; and the establishment of the friendly Chief, Akitoye, with his followers, in the seat of power at Lagos.

By my letter of December 19, 1851, their Lordships are aware that Kosoko very recently rejected the proffered friendship of England, and that he opposed with fire and sword the approach of a flag of truce proceeding to his seat of government with Mr Consul Beecroft, who offered to negotiate and to advise with him, and who was merely attended by an escort of armed boats, scarcely or problematically sufficient for his personal safety among savages.

I therefore determined to send a strong and well-organized force to punish this refractory chief; and having, through the untiring energy and exertions of Mr Beecroft, procured the attendance of Akitoye, and nearly 500 of his followers, near the scene of action, ready to take advantage of a clear sweep when we should make it, I concerted measures with Captain Lewis T. Jones, of the "Sampson", and Captain Henry Lyster, of this ship, who both were volunteers on the occasion, and entrusted the detail and execution of the service to Captain Jones, seconded by Captain Lyster; and their Lordships will see, from the accompanying reports, the complete success with which the enterprise has been crowned.

I am at a loss to do justice to the chivalrous bearing and devoted bravery of these two officers: Captain Jones, who, commanding the expedition, was no less conspicuous for his gallantry and firmness than for his judgement and energy; and Captain Lyster, who, finding himself by unavoidable circumstances, exposed in the "Teazer" to be summarily destroyed by the enemy's guns, made a noble rush into the midst of armed hosts on shore, and, with his undaunted followers, spiked the obnoxious guns and turned the fortune of the day at that point. It is to be borne in mind that our people could expect no quarter; nor did they get any.

I should come short of my duty did I not bring before the notice of their Lordships, the ardent and devoted gallantry exhibited during this very severe affair by officers and men. The responsible post which Captain Lyster filled cost him a severe wound, happily not dangerous; Commander Hillyar, of this ship, who charged with him, is severely but not dangerously wounded; Lieutenants Edward Marshall and T.D. Rich, each in command of a paddlebox-boat, exhibited heroism and firmness never surpassed. Lieutenant John Corbett, in command of Mr Beecroft's iron boat with rockets, with his own hands spiked the guns, receiving a shot in his arm after doing so, and had five severe wounds before the affair ended. Lieutenant Williams, RMA, was dangerously wounded; and Mr Frederick Fletcher, midshipman, commanding one of the cutters appointed to guard the boats when on shore, defended them to the last, and fell with two balls in his forehead. With the other division, Lieutenant Saumarez, of the "Sampson", received a dangerous wound, while encouraging his men; and Mr Richards, midshipman of that ship, got his death-wound.

The conduct of Lieutenant Patey, commanding the "Bloodhound", and Lieutenant Leckie, commanding the "Teazer", and the success attending their efforts, is beyond all praise. Besides their annihilating fire, their vessels were a rallying-point for the respective divisions of boats, and were conspicuously instrumental in the attainment of victory, reflecting infinite credit on all belonging to them. Commander Coote, of the "Volcano", and Commander Gardner, of the "Waterwitch", with their detachments, contributed, as soon as they arrived, to the labours of the hour with an energy and zeal well worthy of them.

Nothing could exceed the devotion of the officers of the medical staff to the exigencies of the day: Mr Richard Carpenter, Surgeon; Mr Walling and Mr Sproule, Assistant Surgeons of this ship; Dr Barclay, Acting Surgeon of the "Sealark"; and Mr Morgan and Mr Pendrith, Assistant Surgeons of the "Sampson". Wherever a man was struck in the boats, a medical officer was immediately by his side, setting their own lives at nought when compared with the wants of their brave companions in arms. Mr Walling and Mr Sproule landed at the charge, with their comrades under Captain Lyster.

Mr Beecroft, during all the operations, was on board the "Bloodhound", and gave every assistance that his advice and experience could afford.

I cannot withhold the expression of my regret for the very severe loss which has attended this achievement, but in which I trust their Lordships will feel that the dignity of England has been asserted and the honour of the flag gloriously sustained.

H.W. BRUCE

Enclosure

Captain Jones to Commodore Bruce
"Bloodhound", off the North Point of Lagos,
(Extract) *December 29, 1851*

In my letter to you dated the 27th, I had the extreme gratification of reporting to you the entire and complete success of the expeditionary forces which you did me the honour of placing under my command, upon which event permit me sincerely to congratulate you.

It now becomes my duty to represent to you in an official form, my proceedings since leaving the "Sampson", and to thank you for allowing me hitherto to keep you acquainted with these movements by private notes as opportunities offered.

In entering into the various details arising from the nature of the service of the several divisions, and to do justice to all, and particularize those who have had the opportunity particularly to distinguish themselves, I feel that I shall be obliged to write rather a long despatch in the form of a daily journal, commencing on the day of my crossing the Bar of Lagos on the 23rd, to the subjugation of our opponents on the 29th December, and finally rejoining you on the 1st January.

You are aware, Sir, that on the 23rd December, in pursuance of your orders to place the "Sampson" in the most advantageous position for throwing shells occasionally across the lagoon, I moored the ship as near as possible at the back of the surf, and then with the boats of the "Sampson", crossed the Bar, preceded by "Bloodhound", and anchored off Point Bruce for the night. On the morning of the 24th, in company with Akitoye and Mr Beecroft, Her Majesty's Consul for the Bights, I mustered and inspected the Badagry and Abbeokutian forces; at the time of muster numbering 500, and increasing during the day to 640. To these we distributed as a mark of recognition, a white neck-tie, with which they seemed much pleased. I then ordered that these men should be supplied with three days' bread from the "Bloodhound".

At 2 PM the "Bloodhound" weighed and crossed to the opposite side of the river, where the boats of the "Sampson", under the orders of Lieutenant T. Saumarez, were sent to launch all the canoes at the slave station on the left bank worth bringing off. At 3 o'clock, Lieutenant Saumarez returned, having in a very short time launched 7 large and 2 small canoes; a most desirable acquisition for the conveyance of the auxiliary forces. The landing party was covered by the guns of the "Bloodhound" right and left, and over-head, to check the advance of an armed force seen from the mast-head advancing. This service being finished, the "Bloodhound" dropped up the river with the tide for the purpose of acquiring piloting knowledge and examining the lines of defence. Three guns from the south end of the island opened on her; the fire was exceedingly well directed, but faulty in elevation. We now knew the channel, and therefore steamed down. At 3.30 PM, true to time and promise, the "Teazer", accompanying the boats of the "Penelope", were seen crossing the Bar; and at 5, "Bloodhound" and "Teazer" anchored near together, out of range of the enemy's shot. Captain Lyster immediately came on board, and placed himself under my orders; we then consulted and decided on the plan of attack, and that the auxiliaries should keep on the right bank of the river, proceeding up as the steam-vessels advanced. The day was too far gone to commence the attack, and we also determined that Christmas Day should be a day of rest; and the 25th was a quiet day, with the exception of the enemy wasting a vast deal of ammunition.

26th. The plan of attack was the suggestion of Captain Lyster, that we should pass the lines of defence as quickly as convenient, and round the north point of the island, and at that point make the grand attack, it being there that Kosoko and the slave-dealers reside, and to let them have the first punishment. The line of sea-defence extends from the south point of the Island of Lagos to the north point along the west front, a distance of nearly two miles, and in parts where the water is sufficiently deep for boats to land, stakes in double rows are driven in six-feet water, and along the whole of this distance an embankment and ditch for the protecting of infantry, and at chosen points, stockades exceedingly strong, made from stout cocoa-nut trees, were erected for guns, the guns being laid for the difficult points of the passage. We could count 4 guns so placed, since found to be 25.

Our work being clear before us, the "Bloodhound" weighed at dawn of day on the 26th, and with the "Sampson's" boats in two divisions, the one preceding, the other following, proceeded up the river; the "Teazer" following with the boats of the "Penelope" similarly arranged, and accompanied by Mr Beecroft's iron-boat "Victoria", fitted for rockets. The enemy immediately opened fire of great guns and musketry, the whole line of embankment being filled with men, the muzzles of the muskets only being visible. This fire was returned from great guns only, and with very beautiful precision, yet with very little effect, for the shot did not do much injury to the green wood of the stockade, and the guns themselves, from being retired, could not be seen.

At 7.20 AM the "Bloodhound" and her division of boats had passed the north-west point, and in trying to get round the north point, grounded in eight feet. The black pilot, John Johns, did his work well and steadily, and is not to blame; the channel had filled up since he was last here— Mr Beecroft and his interpreter, Richards, assisting. We had carried three fathoms all the way up. On sounding it was found impossible to get further. Anchors were therefore laid out to leave off. During this time a very deliberate and beautiful fire was kept up from the 18-pounder of the "Bloodhound", directed by Mr Barry the gunner, and from the 12-pounder howitzer, by Lieutenant McArthur, RMA, with shrapnel and other shells, by which means the great guns abreast were silenced; but nothing could silence the perpetual showers of musketry, the greater part of which fell short, but every now and then one or two would fall on board; and men were hit slightly—very few indeed escaped a slight touch.

The "Teazer" had grounded shortly after weighing, and I did not observe her to be aground before we had advanced too far to anchor for mutual support, as had been agreed upon.

The operations of the division under my immediate direction continued occasionally to throw shot and shell, as any movement was observed on shore, and to check the operations of the enemy, who had nearly succeeded in bringing an invisible gun to bear, the shot at each discharge coming nearer and nearer.

At 10 AM I dispatched Lieutenant Thomas Saumarez in command of the gun-boats of Her Majesty's steamer "Sampson", viz., 1st and 2nd life-boats and pinnace, round the north-east point, to ascertain the strength and position of the guns on that side of the island. A fire from four guns strongly stockaded was immediately opened; this fire was returned from the life-boats and pinnace by the 24 and 12-pounder howitzers with such good effect as to have upset and turned out of its carriage one of these guns. The object being attained of ascertaining the position of the guns on the north-east side of the island, I recalled the boats, as it became requisite to reserve the ammunition and shells for the grand assault, when the other division under Captain Lyster should have joined. The fire from gingals, petrals, and muskets, continuing from the ditch and embankment abreast; and observing the enemy busy in trying to bring other guns into position, I, at 2.30 PM, dispatched Lieutenant T. Saumarez, with the boats of the "Sampson", accompanied by Lieutenant E. McArthur, RMA, in command of the Royal Marine Artillery, to attempt a landing and spike these small guns. They did all that men could do, but it was found impossible to make their way through the showers of musketry opened against them; and Lieutenant Saumarez, therefore, very properly relinquished the attempt, and returned with ten men severely wounded, Mr Richards mortally, and himself hit in three places. I must here bring to your notice the gallant conduct of Mr William J. Stivey, carpenter of Her Majesty's steamer "Sampson", who, neck deep in water, axe in hand, was hewing away at the stakes to make a passage for the boats to land; he is one of those men always where he is wanted. The remainder of the day was passed in firing shot and shell as circumstances required, so as to prevent guns being moved against us; the nearest shots passing about ten yards astern.

27th. At daylight I had the satisfaction of seeing the "Teazer" afloat; and at 7.20, that she had entered the right channel and was coming towards us. I immediately ordered that a deliberate flanking fire should be opened on the west part of the enemy's defences from the "Bloodhound" and gun-boats; and sent a boat, under Mr Bullen, my clerk, to point out to Captain Lyster, the position for the "Teazer" to anchor. 8.10, "Teazer" anchored, and I went on board to see Captain Lyster. Ordered the rocket-boats to take up position to the northward of the "Bloodhound", which was quickly done, and Lieutenant Marshall threw some rockets with beautiful effect, setting fire to several houses, and particularly that of the Prime Minister, Tappa; this produced a spontaneous cheer through the little squadron for the rocket-boat. The rocket-boat shifted her position ahead of the "Teazer", and a general but deliberate fire was opened from the whole force. At 10.45, Lieutenant Marshall threw a rocket, which struck the battery below Tappa's house; and simultaneously, a shot from the "Teazer" capsized the gun. An awful explosion ensued, and from this moment the fate of our foes was decided: it became evident they must submit; house after house caught fire, and the town was shortly in a general blaze. At 10.30, Commander Coote joined, with the boats of the "Volcano", and at 1.45 PM, Commander Gardner, with the boats of the "Waterwitch". At 2.45, I dispatched the gun-boats of the squadron, under Commander Coote, accompanied by the rocket-boat, round the north point, to salute Kosoko's house; but directed that they should only fire a few rounds, being unwilling further to destroy the town; the ultimate fate being positive, should resistance continue. I therefore recalled the boats; sent a summons to Kosoko, by a chief of the Island of Echalli, and determined to wait until Monday morning at 7.

Sunday, 28th. This, on our part, was a day of rest, in preparation for the final assault of the 29th, should Kosoko reject the proffered terms. I felt a reluctance to destroy the detached part of the town still standing, as it would be required for the newcomers. I felt it as a national question, that we should duly observe the Sabbath.

During the whole of this day, canoes from the northeast of Lagos were observed crossing to the Island of Echalli, loaded with furniture and household goods; but I conceived that it was no part of the grand object with which England sent her forces here, to care whether a bed and table, and private property of any kind, were on one side of the river or the other; that might safely be left to the choice of individuals fleeing from a city in flames. I therefore allowed this to go on without molestation, though a jolly-boat might have stopped it. It was also desirable to show that we did not come for pillage, but that our sole object was to stop Slave Trade. At 3.45 PM, it was ascertained that Kosoko and his followers had abandoned the island. I therefore sent my aide-de-camp, Mr Bullen, with the interpreter, Richards, to the chiefs of the auxiliary forces, desiring them to close with the canoes, and escort the rightful King, Akitoye, to his house, and install him in office, preferring that they who had joined him in adversity should have the honour of being his body-guard. None of the British forces landed, except a small party with Commander Coote, to spike guns. In the evening I landed with Captain Lyster and Mr Beecroft, when a scene of the most perfect desolation presented itself.

The lines of defence are the most cunningly devised scheme for entrapping assailants into ambush that can be conceived. I have desired Lieutenant McArthur to make sketches, which shall be forwarded to you when ready.

A creek and swamp, running about 200 yards inland, had checked the flames, and saved the eastern division of the town.

29th. At daylight, I ordered Commander Coote, with his own boats and those of the "Sampson", and Commander Gardner, with his boat and those of the "Penelope", the one on the north-east, the other on the north-west point, to embark or destroy the whole of the guns. They returned at noon, having, by extraordinary exertion, embarked and destroyed fifty-two pieces of ordnance.

Thus, Sir, the Island of Lagos and its dependencies are prostrate before us, ours by the right of conquest, to deal with as might be most expedient. Everyone had fled.

It appears that Kosoko, with about 2,000 followers, had absconded in fifty or sixty canoes. The women and children had been sent away several days before. Akitoye and his followers are in full possession.

I have thus, Sir, arrived at the point when the full and complete accomplishment of your instructions was fulfilled; the climax of your expectations, as conveyed in your first order, placing the gallant and devoted officers and men composing the expeditionary forces under my command, realized.

And I cannot, in terms of adequate import, convey to you how fully I appreciate the cheerful endurance of intense heat, the perpetual rattling of shot from an invisible foe, and the labour of getting the vessels afloat after grounding.

In these duties each and all in their several departments exerted their best; but the toil and anxieties of floating the vessels principally devolved on Lieutenant Russell Patey, of the "Bloodhound", and Lieutenant Leckie, of the "Teazer". Each and all have done their duty with a cheerfulness and good-will worthy of the righteous cause upon which we have been engaged, and to all my best thanks are due.

I herewith send lists of the killed and wounded, amounting to killed, 15; wounded, 75.

I have yet another paragraph to add to this lengthened despatch, which I cannot without extreme injustice omit, and that is, to express how deeply I feel indebted to Mr Rupert H. Bullen, clerk of the "Sampson", who has combined the duties of secretary and aide-de-camp; and when I say that no Lieutenant would have done better, I hope I shall convey to you how fully I appreciate his services.

Lewis T. Jones

Commodore Bruce to the Secretary of the Admiralty
"Penelope", off Lagos, January 3, 1852

Sir,

I transmit herewith, to be laid before the Lords Commissioners of the Admiralty, a letter from Captain Lewis T. Jones, reporting the successful and final termination of the service in the River Lagos, which forms the subject of my despatch to you dated the 2nd instant.

H.W. Bruce

Enclosure

"Sampson", off Lagos, January 1, 1852

Sir,

I have the honour of reporting to you the termination of the proceedings of the expeditionary forces under my command, having at 2 PM to-day recrossed the Bar with the "Bloodhound" and "Teazer", and boats of the "Sampson".

The 30th and 31st December were occupied by Mr Beecroft and myself in visiting the adjacent Island of Echalli, and explaining to the natives the object of the English coming up the river.

That it was solely to "prevent the exportation of slaves". That "the suppression of this abominable Traffic would lead to lawful and free trade". That "England would take all the oil they could make".

They were also told, and told to spread it far and wide, "never to fear an attack from the English, but always come forward and meet them as friends; that we never fired first, but that if people assailed us, we 'hit hard'".

Each of these announcements was received with great joy and clapping of hands; it seemed as if a new existence had opened on these fine-looking athletic men.

On the 31st Akitoye hoisted his flag: white with red cross diagonally.

Akitoye signed the provisional Slave Treaty at the King's house, in the presence of a large concourse of people, the Separate Articles being read aloud and translated by Richards the interpreter, the people approving as each Article was read, by clapping of hands and the peculiar snapping of thumbs.

It is, Sir, with considerable pleasure that I can report to you the perfect state of the health of the crew of the "Sampson"; there is but one man in the list, exclusive of the wounded.

In conclusion, I trust and hope that my own heart, and the hearts of each and every one engaged in the late operations, is fully impressed with the bountiful goodness of God in protecting them from sickness, in cheering them through most laborious duties, and enabling them to do their duty to their noble country with courage and fidelity.

LEWIS T. JONES

Commander Bruce to the Secretary of the Admiralty
"Penelope", off Lagos, January 2, 1852

Sir,

By the accompanying correspondence, the Lords Commissioners of the Admiralty will observe that there is a probability of our obtaining concessions from the King of Dahomey. I have acquainted Commander T.G. Forbes, of the "Philomel", that as soon as His Majesty signs a treaty similar to that which we have with Lagos, stipulating, in addition, that there shall be perpetual peace between Dahomey and Abbeokuta, the blockade of Whydah will be withdrawn, but not before. I am glad to find that the King of Dahomey has so promptly noticed my despatch to him, and I hope, in a very short time to bring all the chiefs between Cape St Paul and the Benin (a line of coast notorious as containing the most extensive slaving establishments in Africa), to agree to the terms which I am directed by Her Majesty's Government to propose to them.

H. W. Bruce

P.S. I highly approve of the promptitude and energy shown by Commander T.G. Forbes in proceeding to Abomey at once.

Enclosure 1
Commander T.G. Forbes to Commodore Bruce
"Philomel", off Whydah, December 31, 1851

Sir,
In a communication dated 26th December, from Vice-Consul L. Fraser, I was under the impression that he only wanted me or one of my officers to go to Abomey, more as a companion than a matter of duty; and as your instructions to me express that on no consideration did you think it advisable for me to land or allow any person under my orders, I therefore declined, particularly as I did not like leaving the brig in charge of Lieutenant Morrell, my Senior Lieutenant being absent at the time.

I have this day received the enclosed letter, dated 30th December, from Thomas Hutton, Esq., which makes it appear to me that I should at once accede to the King of Dahomey's wishes, of being present on this important occasion, and therefore shall proceed early to-morrow with the King's express messengers for Abomey.

THOS. G. FORBES

Enclosure 2

Vice-Consul Fraser to Commander T.G. Forbes
Whydah, December 26, 1851

Sir,

I have just received the King of Dahomey's stick and message, calling me to Abomey. I should like yourself or one of your Lieutenants to accompany me, more particularly as it would be in accordance with the King's wishes.

Things seem to be going on favourably, but I fear the sacrifices will be the great obstacle.

L. FRASER
HBM's Vice-Consul in Dahomey

Enclosure 3

Mr Hutton to Commander T. G. Forbes
Whydah, December 30, 1851

Sir,

The Yavogau and chiefs of this town, with express messengers from the King of Dahomey, have called upon me to request that I shall endeavour to prevail upon you to favour the King with an interview at Dahomey.

Mr Vice-Consul Fraser, who left for Dahomey last evening, informed me that in accordance with your instructions, it was not conceived advisable that yourself should visit the shore; and such intimation I am led to infer has been made known to the King, who appears most anxious that yourself, being Her Majesty's Senior Officer on this station, should be present on this important occasion, the effecting a treaty for the suppression of the Slave Trade.

The Yavogau and chiefs, the Da Souzas and the principal residents here, with Senhor Domingo Martinez of Porto Novo, and also myself, are invited to be present.

I am assured the King will feel much aggrieved if disappointed in the favour of your presence; permit me to hope that you will gratify him, as your presence will certainly tend to lessen difficulties, and dispose him to bring this long-desired treaty to a successful conclusion.

T. HUTTON

Consul Beecroft to Viscount Palmerston (received February 16)
"Bloodhound", off Lagos, January 3, 1852

(Extract)

Thursday, January 1, 1852. 9 o'clock, King Akitoye and his two chiefs arrived. 10.15, weighed, and proceeded. 12 o'clock, anchored inside of the Bar. 2.30, weighed, and proceeded across; "Teazer" in company astern; anchored near Her Majesty's steamer "Penelope". Akitoye and chiefs accompanied me on board of flag-ship; a salute was fired from Her Majesty's brig "Waterwitch", on account of wounded on board of "Penelope". They were very kindly received by the Commodore, and invited below to the after-cabin. The Treaty was signed—the original I herewith enclose. After a short conference they took their leave in the flag-ship's cutter, and crossed; a large canoe was in waiting within the Bar.

I trust what has been done will meet with your Lordship's approbation. I beg leave to state I write these proceedings in great haste, to go by Her Majesty's steamer "Sampson". As I close this despatch, "Philomel's" boat arrived from off Whydah, with a letter to the Commodore from Commander Forbes of the above-mentioned vessel, stating that Guezo, the King of Dahomey, had requested Vice-Consul Fraser, with a naval officer, to proceed to

Abomey: Commander Forbes has accordingly followed Mr Fraser. It appears he is anxious at once to enter into a treaty; if so, the blockade and the conquest of Lagos has had some effect in changing his policy in two or three days; for in a brief note from Vice-Consul Fraser, dated the 23rd ultimo, he stated his liberty was stopped for a day or two.

JOHN BEECROFT

Enclosure
Engagement with the King and Chiefs of Lagos

Engagement between Her Majesty the Queen of England and the King and Chiefs of Lagos, for the abolition of the Traffic in Slaves. Signed at Lagos, on board HMS "Penelope", on the 1st day of January, 1852.

Commodore Henry William Bruce, Commander-in-Chief of Her Majesty's ships and vessels on the west coast of Africa, and John Beecroft, Esq., Her Majesty's Consul in the Bights of Benin and Biafra, on the part of Her Majesty the Queen of England, and the King and Chiefs of Lagos and of the neighbourhood, on the part of themselves and of their country, have agreed upon the following:

ARTICLE I
The export of slaves to foreign countries is for ever abolished in the territories of the King and Chiefs of Lagos; and the King and Chiefs of Lagos engage to make and to proclaim a law prohibiting any of their subjects, or any person within their jurisdiction, from selling or assisting in the sale of any slave for transportation to a foreign country; and the King and Chiefs of Lagos promise to inflict a severe punishment on any person who shall break this law.

ARTICLE II
No European or other person whatever shall be permitted to reside within the territory of the King and Chiefs of

Lagos for the purpose of carrying on in any way the Traffic in Slaves; and no houses, or stores, or buildings of any kind whatever, shall be erected for the purpose of Slave Trade within the territory of the King and Chiefs of Lagos; and if any such houses, stores, or buildings shall at any future time be erected, and the King and Chiefs of Lagos shall fail or be unable to destroy them, they may be destroyed by any British officers employed for the suppression of Slave Trade.

ARTICLE III
If at any time it shall appear that Slave Trade has been carried on through or from the territory of the King and Chiefs of Lagos, the Slave Trade may be put down by Great Britain by force upon that territory, and British officers may seize the boats of Lagos found anywhere carrying on the Slave Trade; and the King and Chiefs of Lagos will be subject to a severe act of displeasure on the part of the Queen of England.

ARTICLE IV
The slaves now held for exportation shall be delivered up to any British officer duly authorized to receive them, for the purpose of being carried to a British colony, and there liberated; and all the implements of Slave Trade, and the barracoons, or buildings exclusively used in the Slave Trade, shall be forthwith destroyed.

ARTICLE V
Europeans or other persons now engaged in the Slave Trade, are to be expelled the country; the houses, stores, or buildings hitherto employed as slave factories, if not converted to lawful purposes within three months of the conclusion of this Engagement, are to be destroyed.

ARTICLE VI
The subjects of the Queen of England may always trade freely with the people of Lagos in every article they may

wish to buy and sell in all the places, and ports, and rivers within the territories of the King and Chiefs of Lagos, and throughout the whole of their dominions; and the King and Chiefs of Lagos pledge themselves to show no favour, and give no privilege to the ships and traders of other countries, which they do not show to those of England.

ARTICLE VII

The King and Chiefs of Lagos declare that no human beings shall, at any time, be sacrificed within their territories, on account of religious or other ceremonies; and that they will prevent the barbarous practice of murdering prisoners captured in war.

ARTICLE VIII

Complete protection shall be afforded to missionaries, or ministers of the Gospel, of whatever nation or country, following their vocation of spreading the knowledge and doctrines of Christianity, and extending the benefits of civilization within the territory of the King and Chiefs of Lagos. Encouragement shall be given to such missionaries or ministers in the pursuits of industry, in building houses for their residence, and schools and chapels. They shall not be hindered or molested in their endeavours to teach the doctrines of Christianity to all persons willing and desirous to be taught; nor shall any subjects of the King and Chiefs of Lagos, who may embrace the Christian faith, be, on that account, or on account of the teaching or exercise thereof, molested or troubled in any manner whatsoever. The King and Chiefs of Lagos further agree to set apart a piece of land, within a convenient distance of the principal towns, to be used as a burial-ground for Christian persons. And the funerals and sepulchres of the dead shall not be disturbed in any way or upon any account.

Article IX

Power is hereby expressly reserved to the Government of France to become a party to this Treaty, if it shall think fit, agreeably with the provision contained in the Vth Article of the Convention between Her Majesty and the King of the French for the suppression of the Traffic in Slaves, signed at London, May 29, 1845.

In faith of which we have hereunto set our hands and seals, at Lagos, on board HBM ship "Penelope", this 1st day of January, 1852.

H.W. Bruce   KING AKITOYE X (his mark)
JOHN BEECROFT   ATCHOBOO X (his mark)
                              KOSAE X (his mark)

Witnesses:
LEWIS T. JONES, *Captain, HMS "Sampson"*
H. LYSTER, *Captain, HMS "Penelope"*
W. HICKMAN, *Secretary to Commander-in-Chief*

Commodore Bruce to the Secretary of the Admiralty
"Penelope", Ascension, January 17, 1852

Sir,

The recent operations in the Bight of Benin which were undertaken in compliance with instructions from the Lords of the Admiralty, will, there is every reason to suppose, be the means of stopping the Slave Trade in that portion of Africa. The expulsion of the white slave-dealers from Lagos, the deposition of its barbarous Chief, Kosoko, and the establishment of a friendly and comparatively civilized ruler in his place, has opened out a field for legitimate commercial enterprise to an extent difficult to define.

Lagos, lately an excellent and well-built native town, situated near to the sea-coast on the bank of a river which is accessible to vessels drawing as much as ten or eleven feet, and having water-communication far into the interior beyond Abbeokuta, and for hundreds of miles along the coast, appears to be natural magazine for such of the produce of the surrounding country as is intended for exportation. The natives are a brave and intelligent race, and more desirous of partaking of the comforts and luxuries consequent on an intercourse with European traders, than most of the adjacent tribes. Their exports of palm-oil and ivory under the late Government were very considerable, and now, when they perceive that their favourite occupation of slave-dealing must from the strict blockade which is kept up by the British cruizers, be relinquished, and are made to understand that their topographical position enables them to become the carriers of merchandise to and from the inland nations, it may be supposed that they would, with a proper degree of management, turn their attention to lawful pursuits, and before long be the wealthiest and most considerable people in Western Africa.

But unfortunately, the Traffic in Slaves is of all descriptions of commerce, the one most congenial to the habits and disposition of the African: the marauding expeditions undertaken at certain seasons for the capture of slaves, establish his character for enterprise and courage among his brethren; the boundless and cruel control he exercises over his captives in the barracoons is gratifying to his savage temper; and the readiness with which he finds purchasers for them satisfies his cupidity. Experience shows us that he will never voluntarily abandon this vile Traffic.

At this moment our negotiations with Dahomey are progressing to a favourable termination; the petty chiefs in the Bight of Benin will be governed by the result. Lagos, the greatest slave emporium, is in our power, and the people are ready to accede to any terms which we may propose to them; but the difficulty is in keeping them to their engagements. The Slave Trade requires no organized system for its support; it might cease for a century and be renewed in a week; remove the blockading squadron, and to-morrow, if the Spaniards or Brazilians were willing to buy slaves, the chiefs would be ready to sell them, notwithstanding their pledges to the contrary. Still there are, in my opinion, means, by the adoption of which, the squadron might, to effect all that is required of it on this point, be reduced to a number only sufficient to watch over the interests of legitimate traders, namely, by establishing Consuls and Agents at different places, whose duty it should be to ascertain whether or not the native chiefs to whom they are accredited, faithfully observe their engagements for the abolition of the Slave Trade. They should be instructed to foster legitimate commerce, to keep up a constant communication with the officers commanding Her Majesty's ships; to impart at once any intelligence they might obtain of a breach of treaty, and the offending chief should be summarily punished for the same by the stoppage of trade and the destruction of his coast town. It should be their duty to report to the Senior Naval Officer, for the information of Her Majesty's Government, once a month at least, the state of affairs within the limits of their respective Consulates or Agencies; they should be strictly forbidden to interfere in the political concerns of the countries in which they are residing, and prohibited from entering into commercial speculations, either on their own account or on account of other parties. The persons best adapted for these situations would be intelligent and fairly educated Creoles of the West Indies, or natives of Sierra Leone, as they alone are capable of withstanding the effects of the climate. I would suggest that on the respective chiefs entering into anti-Slave Trade engagements, Consuls be appointed at Lagos and Whydah, and Agents at Elmina Chica, Fish Town, Ahguay, Great Popo, Appi, Porto Novo, Badagry, Jacknah, Jabor and the Oddi.

If the Consuls at Lagos and Whydah were to be paid 300*l.* a-year each, and the Agents at the other ports above mentioned 200*l.* a-year each, the charge would amount to 2,600*l.* a-year, being one-fourth less than the expense of a 6-gun brig. Three cruizers would be sufficient, instead of seven, the number now required; and thus a saving would be effected of nearly 20,000*l.* a-year, and the objects of Her Majesty's Government more likely to be accomplished than by an adherence to the present system.

The trade in the Bight of Biafra is so considerable, that I am sure Mr Beecroft would be fully and most usefully occupied in confining his attention to British interests in that quarter; and I should therefore recommend his being relieved of the duties arising in those parts of his Consulate which are situated to the westward of the River Benin.

I request you will be pleased to bring this despatch under the notice of their Lordships.

H. W. Bruce

Earl of Granville to Consul Beecroft
Foreign Office, January 24, 1852

Sir,
I have received your despatch of the 26th of November last, stating what passed at your conference with Kosoko, the Chief of Lagos, on the 20th of that month, and reporting the circumstances of the attack which you authorized Commander Forbes to make upon the town of Lagos, after Kosoko had rejected your proposal that he should conclude a Treaty with Great Britain for the abolition of the Slave Trade.

I have to acquaint you that Her Majesty's Government are of opinion that you were not borne out, either by the circumstances of the case, or by your instructions from Her Majesty's Government, in directing that Her Majesty's naval forces should land and attack Lagos; and Her Majesty's Government greatly regret the loss of life which has been the consequence of that attack.

The latest instruction which you had received from Viscount Palmerston with reference to the object of your visit to Lagos, was contained in a despatch from his Lordship dated the 21st of February, 1851. That despatch stated, that if the Chief of Lagos should refuse to abandon the Slave Trade and to expel the slave-traders, you were to remind him of the presence on the coasts of his territory of a powerful British squadron, and of the fact that his authority had been founded on an usurpation; but you were not directed to resort immediately to hostilities against Kosoko: and Her Majesty's Government cannot but regret that you did not, after the unsatisfactory termination of your conference with Kosoko, determine to wait till you should have had an opportunity of conferring with Commodore Bruce as to the nature of the coercive measures proper to be adopted against Lagos.

I am aware that Lord Palmerston's despatch to you of the 11th of October, 1850, enclosed a copy of a letter to the Admiralty of the same date, stating that it appeared to his Lordship, that if the Chief of Lagos should refuse to enter into an engagement similar to that which was agreed to by the Chiefs of Gallinas, measures similar to those which were enforced against Gallinas should be brought to bear upon Lagos; but you should have borne in mind that the Commander-in-Chief of Her Majesty's Naval Forces on the west coast of Africa was the only person who could properly direct any measures to be taken with reference to that letter; and if you had consulted Commodore Bruce before you proceeded to require Commander Forbes to attack Lagos, hostile measures might have been avoided; and if a necessity had subsequently arisen for the employment of force, instead of directing against the Chief of Lagos an unsuccessful attack, which will necessitate further hostilities to do away with the bad moral effect which has been produced upon the natives, such precautions might have been taken as would have ensured success.

I regret to be obliged to disapprove of your conduct in this affair, as Her Majesty's Government have had occasion to remark on the zeal and activity with which you have generally carried out the instructions given by Her Majesty's Government with the view to put an end to the Slave Trade.

GRANVILLE

FEBRUARY 1852

Mr Layard to the Secretary of the Admiralty
Foreign Office, February 23, 1852

Sir,

I have laid before Earl Granville copies of despatches from Commodore Bruce, the Commander-in-Chief of Her Majesty's Naval Forces on the west coast of Africa, and from Captains Jones and Lyster, reporting their proceedings in the attack which was made upon the Island and Town of Lagos on the 26th and 27th of December last, and which compelled the usurper Kosoko to evacuate that town with his forces, and led to the restoration of Akitoye, the rightful Sovereign of Lagos.

The great numerical strength of the enemy, the entrenchments by which they had skilfully fortified the place and its approaches, and the natural difficulties attending the ascent of the river, rendered this expedition peculiarly arduous and formidable; and Lord Granville feels called upon to say, that it appears to him that the officers and men engaged in the reduction of Lagos have greatly distinguished themselves, and have fully maintained the high and well-earned reputation of the British Navy for courage and gallantry; and if the Lords of the Admiralty should concur in this opinion, Lord Granville hopes that Commodore Bruce may receive from their Lordships a suitable acknowledgement of the distinguished services of the officers and men employed under his orders in this action.

A. H. LAYARD

Earl Granville to Consul Beecroft
Foreign Office, February 23, 1852

Sir,

It was my duty to inform you by my despatch of the 24th ultimo, that Her Majesty's Government were of opinion that you were not justified in requiring Commander T. G. Forbes, of Her Majesty's steamer "Philomel", to direct against the town of Lagos the attack which was made by the boats of Her Majesty's squadron on the 25th of November last; and I have since learnt from the Admiralty, that the view which I took of these transactions on the receipt of your despatch of the 26th of November, has been fully borne out by the opinion thereupon which Commodore Bruce communicated to Commander Forbes on the 19th of December, after having investigated upon the spot all that occurred on that occasion.

I have now to acknowledge the receipt of your despatch of the 3rd of January, reporting your proceedings on board Her Majesty's steamer "Bloodhound", between the 30th of November, 1851, and the 1st of January last; and I have to acquaint you that Her Majesty's Government have learnt with great satisfaction that the formidable resistance of the King and chiefs of Lagos has been completely subdued by the skill and intrepidity so eminently displayed by Her Majesty's Naval Forces under Captain Jones, in the attack upon that island and town, on the 26th and 27th of December.

I have no doubt that by your professional and local knowledge, and by your perseverance and activity, you have been enabled to render important services to Commodore Bruce, in preparing and carrying into execution his plans for the attack upon Lagos; and I hope that the restoration of the rightful chief, Akitoye, to his sovereignty, combined with the signature of the Treaty which he concluded with Commodore Bruce and you on the 1st of January, may lead to the complete extirpation of the Slave Trade from the stronghold which it has found for some years at Lagos.

I have the gratification of informing you that Her Majesty's Government have confirmed the Treaty of the 1st of January, and that they entirely approve the part taken by you in the proceedings of Her Majesty's squadron since the 30th of November last.

GRANVILLE

Other titles in the series

The Amritsar Massacre: General Dyer in the Punjab, 1919

"We feel that General Dyer, by adopting an inhuman and un-British method of dealing with subjects of His Majesty the King-Emperor, has done great disservice to the interest of British rule in India. This aspect it was not possible for the people of the mentality of General Dyer to realise."

Backdrop

At the time of the events described, India was under British rule. Indians had fought alongside the British in World War I, and had made tremendous financial contributions to the British war effort. Mahatma Gandhi was the leader of the Indian National Congress party, which was seeking independence from the British Empire.

The Book

This is the story of the action taken by Brigadier-General Dyer at Amritsar in the Punjab in 1919. Faced with insurrection in support of Mahatma Gandhi, the British Army attempted to restore order. General Dyer, on arriving in the troubled city of Amritsar, issued an order banning any assembly of more than four people. Consequently, when he discovered a large crowd gathered together during a cattle fair, he took the astonishing action of shooting more than three hundred unarmed people. Regarding the subsequent native obedience as a satisfactory result, he was surprised to find himself removed from command a year later, and made lengthy representations to Parliament.

ISBN 0 11 702412 0   Price £6.99

The Siege of the Peking Embassy, 1900

"I cannot conclude this despatch without saying a word of praise respecting the ladies of all nationalities who so ably and devotedly assisted the defence, notwithstanding the terrible shadow which at all times hung over the legation—a shadow which the never-ceasing rattle of musketry and crash of round shot and shell and the diminishing number of defenders rendered ever present. They behaved with infinite patience and cheerfulness, helping personally in the hospital or, in making sandbags and bandages, and in assisting in every possible way the work of defence. Especially commended are two young ladies—Miss Myers and Miss Daisy Brazier—who daily filtered the water for the hospital, in tropical heat, and carried it with bullets whistling and shells bursting in the trees overhead."   Sir Claude MacDonald

The Backdrop

The Boxer movement in China was a secret society which preached hatred of foreigners. By the spring of 1900, this movement was out of control. On 9 June, the Boxers launched their first attack against foreign property in Peking by burning down the racecourse. On 19 June, all foreigners were ordered to evacuate Peking within 24 hours. The order was not complied with.

The Book

As events worsened for the diplomats and their families in Peking, Sir Claude MacDonald, the British ambassador, wired the Admiralty in Taku to request the immediate despatch of a relief force. Just how that relief force fared, and how the hundreds of diplomats and their families who were stranded inside the Legation buildings coped with the rigours of the siege, are the subject of the diplomatic papers presented in this book. The central part of the story is the gripping diary of events kept by Sir Claude MacDonald.

ISBN 0 11 702456 2   Price £6.99

Florence Nightingale and the Crimea, 1854–55

"By an oversight, no candles were included among the stores brought to the Crimea. Lamps and wicks were brought but not oil. These omissions were not supplied until after possession had been taken of Balaklava, and the purveyor had an opportunity of purchasing candles and oil from the shipping and the dealers in the town."

Backdrop
The British Army arrived in the Crimea in 1854, ill-equipped to fight a war in the depths of a Russian winter.

The Book
The hospital service for wounded soldiers during the Crimean War was very poor and became the subject of concern, not just in the army, but also in the press. "The Times" was publishing letters from the families of soldiers describing the appalling conditions. This embarrassed the government, but even more it irritated the army, which did not know how to cope with such open scrutiny of its activities.

The book is a collection of extracts from government papers published in 1855 and 1856. Their selection provides a snapshot of events at that time. In particular they focus on the terrible disaster that was the Charge of the Light Brigade, and the inadequate provisions that were made for the care of the sick and wounded. The documents relating to the hospitals at Scutari include evidence from Florence Nightingale herself.

ISBN 0 11 702425 2   Price £6.99

Lord Kitchener and Winston Churchill: The Dardanelles Commission Part I, 1914–15

"The naval attack on the Narrows was never resumed. It is difficult to understand why the War Council did not meet between 19th March and 14th May. The failure of the naval attack showed the necessity of abandoning the plan of forcing the passage of the Dardanelles by purely naval operation. The War Council should then have met and considered the future policy to be pursued."

Backdrop

The Dardanelles formed part of the main southern shipping route to Russia, and was of great military and strategic importance to whoever controlled it. However, it had long been recognised by the British naval and military authorities that any attack on the Dardanelles would be an operation fraught with great difficulties.

The Book

During the early stages of World War I, Russia made a plea to her allies to make a demonstration against the Turks. So attractive was the prize of the Dardanelles to the British generals, notably Lord Kitchener, that this ill-fated campaign was launched. Just how powerful an influence Kitchener was to exert over the War Council, and just how ill-prepared the Allies were to conduct such an attack, are revealed in dramatic detail in the report of this Commission.

The book covers the first part of the Commission's report. It deals with the origin, inception and conduct of operations in the Dardanelles from the beginning of the war in August 1914 until March 1915, when the idea of a purely naval attack was abandoned.

ISBN 0 11 702423 6   Price £6.99

Defeat at Gallipoli: The Dardanelles Commission Part II, 1915–16

"It has been represented ... that from a military point of view, the Dardanelles Expedition, even if unsuccessful, was justified by the fact that it neutralised or contained a large number of Turkish troops who otherwise would have been free to operate elsewhere. Lord Kitchener estimated this number as being nearly 300,000. But in containing the Turkish force, we employed ... a total of at least 400,000. Our casualties amounted to 31,389 killed, 78,749 wounded and 9,708 missing, making a total of 119,846. The expedition also involved heavy financial expenditure and the employment of a considerable naval force."

Backdrop
The naval attempt by the British to force the Dardanelles was abandoned in March 1915. Rather than losing face, the military commanders decided to send a large army to the area.

The Book
Picking up the story from where the earlier volume, *Lord Kitchener and Winston Churchill* left off, this second part of the Dardanelles Commission's report deals with the disastrous military campaign to capture the Gallipoli Peninsula using ground forces. As the story unfolds, we learn how the Allies were unable to make any headway against an enemy who was well prepared and well positioned. Within a few months the Allies had suffered a humiliating defeat, and thousands of men had lost their lives. The realisation of the government's incompetence in handling this affair was instrumental in the removal of Herbert Asquith as Prime Minister in December 1916.

ISBN 0 11 702455 4   Price £6.99